D1516474

DECENTRALIZED FINANCE (DEFI) FOR BEGINNERS

DEFI AND BLOCKCHAIN, BORROW, LEND, TRADE, SAVE & INVEST IN PEER TO PEER LENDING & FARMING

NICK WOODS

PUBLISHING FORTE

INTRODUCTION

Life can be unpredictable and challenging at times, as every individual out there has to find a way to earn money to provide for themselves and their family. In our day-to-day life, we all have countless duties to look forward to, to ensure that we can be stable. With the rise of Covid 19 and its huge impact on the entire globe, countless large corporations and companies around the world focused on one main thing, and that is money and how it should be generated amongst the population for maximum profit and value.

After considerations and planning, many people were introduced to the idea of decentralized finance and started to grasp its importance and benefits. You might be wondering what exactly is decentralized finance and why many people have jumped on to this mega topic?

Well, to put it simply, decentralized finance is a form of unique financial technology that allows every individual, regardless of status, location, and background, to transfer funds without the need of a middle organization or company such as a bank or any other financial institutions that work to control money. The main purpose and idea behind decentralized finance are to remove the idea of having banks and financial institutions control and regulate money but instead give individuals the opportunity to store their financial assets/money in a secure digital wallet.

Now, if you are new to this whole idea of decentralized finance, you might be wondering what exactly its purpose is and why many people around the world prefer and rely on this digital financial system rather than the traditional banking system.

Well, the answer to that is quite simple and plain, which is that with the help of decentralized finance, users do not have to pay a fixed rate of fee that other large well-known banks and corporations charge. Besides this, individuals also have an equal opportunity to transfer personal money within minutes without requiring the need for approval.

When we talk about third party involvement, local banks in your area use them to create a platform where you have to go through a rather strenuous and long process; however, with the introduction of decentralized finance and its components such as stable coins, software, and hardware, individuals are easily able to access and store their personal money and are able to transfer it easily without involvement from third parties. If you are someone who is confused by the idea of decentralized finance, it is best that you first understand centralized finance to have a better understanding further.

When focusing on the aspects of centralized finance, you should know that your money or any other financial assets are being held and under the supervision of a large corporation such as a bank, and in return for the services they provide you,

you have to pay them. For example, let's assume that you go to a grocery store to buy a gallon of water, so when you purchase it with a credit card, the charge itself goes to an acquiring bank of the credit card, and from there, the information is forwarded to the credit card network.

As the network clears the charge, it in return asks for a payment from the bank, and as the bank approves the charge and sends a receipt to the network, you will be charged a fee since you are using their services. On the other hand, decentralized finance eliminates the need to have a loop of third parties/brokers/banks, etc., to secure your financial assets and money but rather allows you to conduct financial transactions in businesses with the help of its emerging safe technology.

By having a secure and working internet connection, you can transfer, borrow, lend, and much more using decentralized finance technology. As you are using its services, the software is designed to record and store all the information for safety and reliability reasons. Furthermore, if you are unaware, you should know that one of the most common and popular cryptocurrencies, Bitcoin is itself decentralized money as there is no involvement of local banks and organizations during transactional processes.

We as humans use different varieties of services that make up our financial system, for instance, saving plans, loans, insurance, etc. All of these things are connected by money, and to maximize its use, we get help from banks and organizations that charge us a service fee; however, there are certain risks involved under this centralized financial system, such as fraud, mismanagement, corruption, and much more. For this and other major reasons that we will talk about in detail throughout the book, many individuals are starting to familiarize themselves with decentralized finance to fully secure their funds.

Let's start with the first chapter of the book that talks about decentralized finance in further detail to help you understand its importance in not only your everyday life but also for businesses and large corporations which use heavy money.

1

UNDERSTANDING DEFI

Many people out there think and believe that it is quite difficult to understand and use decentralized finance, but in reality, it is the opposite as any individual, regardless of their income, knowledge, place, and standard, can get tremendous benefits out of DeFi. When it comes to the basic definition of decentralized finance, it can be said that it is simply a form of financial services which does not include any form of central authority, whether it be a person or a well-known company/organization.

WHEN INDIVIDUALS USE DECENTRALIZED money such as Bitcoin or any other cryptocurrency popular in the stock market, they are able to create a secondary business that involves exchanges, lending services, insurance services, and much more that do not have any owner and are not centrally controlled by any person or firm. Let's look at, in detail, the components of decentralized finance and how you can get started.

History of Decentralizing Finance

To start from the beginning, although there was no one agreed-upon date when decentralized finance was born, there were, however, a few important events that made DeFi possible. The first of them was the creation of Bitcoin in 2009 by Satoshi Nakamoto.

DESPITE WHETHER BITCOIN should be classified as DeFi or not, its inception was the key enabler for the whole cryptocurrency industry, which decentralized finance, is part of. Bitcoin also allows for sending payments around the world in a decentralized fashion, and payments are one of the areas of finance that looks like DeFi. However, most importantly, Bitcoin allowed a space for the creation of Ethereum, a default blockchain for all the top decentralized finance protocols.

Now, sending Bitcoin around the world is extremely beneficial and a unique way to have advancements in the finance sector. The finance does not stop there as every robust financial system needs a set of other important services such as lending, borrowing, trading funding, or derivatives. Bitcoin, with its limited and relatively simple language called script, was just not suitable for these kinds of applications. Script limitations were one of the most important factors that contributed to the creation of Ethereum by Vitalic Buterin. Ethereum began its roots when it was initially launched in 2015 and quickly started attracting more and more developers who wanted to build all kinds of decentralized applications ranging from games such as crypto kitties to finding the actual applications. Ethereum, with its true and complete programming language solidity and the ERC20 standard for creating new tokens, quickly became a go-to smart contract platform to build on.

Components of Decentralized Finance

So now that you know what decentralized finance is let's look at the most important aspect of it all, which is its individual components that make up for the overall workings of this financial system. So in DeFi, you need to have a decentralized infrastructure that allows smooth programming and for running the services, it offers to individuals.

FOR EXAMPLE, you could use a platform that is widely known in the gaming industry market called Ethereum. Ethereum, when linked with DeFi, can be used to digitally write automated code which has another name called smart contracts. Now what this means is that you, being the user of DeFi, have the power to determine the rules as to how a certain service will work and operate.

SO ONCE YOU have deployed those rules on the Ethereum network, you no longer have control over them as they become immutable. Once you have a system in place like Ethereum for creating a decentralized app, you can easily move on to building your own decentralized financial system. After you are done with it, you would need a list of building blocks that you could use to operate a decentralized financial system.

NOW IT IS obvious that the first thing any financial system needs is money, and you may be thinking, why not use Bitcoin, which in theory is a currency. Well, the reason for this is though it is indeed decentralized, it has only very basic programmable functionality and is not entirely compatible with the Ethereum platform. Ether, on the other hand, is compatible and programmable; however, it is also highly volatile. If you are someone who is looking to build reliable financial services that people want to use, you will need a more stable currency within this system, such as stable coins.

Bankings vs. DeFi

To better understand DeFi or decentralized finance, let's take a look at Cefi or centralized finance. In the traditional financial system or centralized finance, if you would like to send your money to somebody else, you are likely going to use some sort of an app such as Venmo or PayPal, or you are going to use a credit card such as a visa or MasterCard.

So in order to do this, it has to go first to your bank, and from there, it goes through the third-party app, then it goes to the Bank of the receiver, and then the receiver finally receives this money. So this shows that third-party centralized intermediaries are included and used in order to conduct a transaction; however, on the other hand, with decentralized finance or DeFi for short, you basically send your money directly to the person with no centralized authority.

Another point worth mentioning is that centralized finance requires trusted centralized intermediaries like the banks or the third-party apps, and not only that, but they also have batch clearing and settlement. Generally, though, there are higher fees and a costly infrastructure attached to a centralized financial system, but this is something you are not required to expect with decentralized finance as the majority of this is all built on a blockchain protocol and hence there are little to no intermediaries required. The main advantage of this is that it allows for faster processing and management and also allows users to have lower fees in a reduced infrastructure cost.

Main benefits of DeFi

When it comes to Decentralized Finance, there are multiple benefits from which users of all ages, backgrounds, understandings, and standards could benefit. The Main benefit to DeFi is that it is open to everyone in the public and is completely anonymous to ensure maximum safety, flexibility, speed, as well as transparency.

NOW YOU MIGHT BE WONDERING what does open mean, and to answer your question, it simply means that you do not need to apply for an account as you can just create a wallet in a matter of minutes. If you are someone who is unsure and are concerned about your personal information, you have nothing to worry about as DeFi is anonymous, which simply means that you do not have to provide any personal information in order to set up an account.

THE THIRD THING is it's flexible, which means that you being the user can move your assets anywhere at any time without asking for permission, such as contacting an organization or company on the phone or paying expensive fees. In addition to that, DeFi is extremely fast, unlike traditional banking systems.

. . .

FOR INSTANCE, if you need something to be done, you essentially have to call somebody on the phone or have to apply for a loan which will make you go through all sorts of paperwork and headache. With decentralized finance, you are allowed to do things such as getting a loan or simply borrowing money.

Stable Coins

In order to understand the workings of a decentralized financial system, you have to familiarize yourself with stable coins and how they work in relation to your spending. Now, you might be wondering; what do stable coins have to do with DeFi and what aspects make stable coins relevant?

STABLE COINS such as Tether and USD coins are all cryptocurrency tokens that are used to bridge decentralized finance with centralized finance. So, for instance, when you buy one stable coin for $1, a new USD coin is minted, and later when you withdraw it, 1 USD coin is burned so that the coin is always worth one United States dollar.

The purpose of this is to have a reliable way to buy and sell certain coins without having to buy and sell them, but instead, you can simply trade them. Let's look at another example for understanding; let's say you bought 1 Ethereum at $500, and after some time, the price of it has risen to $1000 and so you want to sell because you think it is high enough for you to make noticeable Profits.

WITHOUT ACQUIRING the help of stable coins, you would essentially have to sell your Ethereum at a centralized exchange like Coin-base or Binance, and in return, they will give you United States dollars for it, but they are going to take a cut of that transaction. Now let's say after some time, the value of that Ethereum you bought fluctuates, and so you decide to sell them on centralized finance. By doing this, you will notice that after waiting for a few days; you will be able to get money in your account without tackling all the steps you would if you were to sell it without stable coins. Now, this essentially means that with the help of stable coins used with DeFi, you do not have to go through multiple stages of work to exchange your Ethereum.

So that is all for this chapter, folks! Let's head over to the second chapter of the book, which talks all about the main differences between the traditional financial systems and that of Decentralized finance. So without further ado, let's dive in.

DIFFERENTIATING TRADITIONAL FINANCIAL SYSTEM WITH DEFI

I n the previous chapter of this book, we went through understanding the real concept of decentralized finance and how popular it has managed to be amongst many individuals around the world. If you are new to the whole concept of decentralized finance, you might have been wondering about how DeFi managed to cross traditional forms of the financial system that include the use of services of banks and other financial institutions.

WHEN IT COMES to managing your financial situation, there are factors to consider, and for each one of them comes a service fee that you have to pay. Although this form of fund-flow is not entirely wrong as it is a business, the main reason why many people have shifted into DeFi is that besides being relatively cheap, it is also quick and efficient, providing people less time as compared to traditional financial services.

. . .

IN THIS CHAPTER, we will be taking a look at some of the main differences between the traditional financial system and DeFi and compare how important these are. So without any further delay, let's start this chapter.

Rise of Decentralized Finance

When it comes to decentralized finance, it can be seen as an alternative and effective tool for the purpose of financial funds. The overall world DeFi began to grow back in mid-2019 when fifteen Ethereum based projects came together with a goal to create a form of financial building/system that is not only independent and open for everyone but is also safe and quick.

SINCE THERE IS no third-party involvement, the transactions/exchanges made with decentralized finance and stable coins are done easily with a much larger profit in return. Perhaps one of the most striking features that make this form of the financial system stand out the most from the traditional kind is the improvement of operational risks and extra functionality.

SO FAR, we are aware that decentralized finance uses cryptocurrency and smart coins. Although, the real question that stands out is at what cost and limit? Well, the answer to that is a smart one as the cryptocurrency used in addition to DeFi allows users to make fast and quick exchanges without requiring the help or workings of a bank or any other financial institution.

IF YOU ARE someone who has started to use decentralized finance, you will be surprised to see the option of having a peer-to-peer borrow and lending. Since your finance is secure, you can easily exchange cryptocurrency 24/7 in a matter of minutes.

DeFi as a Financial System

Whether you are someone who is new to the whole concept and world of decentralized finance or is someone who actively engages with it, one thing that you might want to know is its pros and what makes it stand out when put beside the traditional finance system that currently is being used by the world; such as banks, third parties and other institutions/corporations come to mind, which can increase the overall span of time to get anything done such as loan payments, transfers, etc.

HOWEVER, DeFi uses the latest blockchain technology, which solely acts as a source of trust. When comparing traditional finance with DeFi, it can be concluded that with traditional finance, there are many entry-level barriers involved, which include regulators, proper licensing, paperwork, and so much more that leaves this overall form of financial system complicated and little scope for any innovation.

BESIDES THIS, another important reason why DeFi has been able to gain its popularity is that it removes bans and barriers imposed by financial institutions. These bans and strict restrictions cause damage to overseas companies and businesses looking to invest, thus causing failures.

OVERALL THOUGH, decentralized finance has been able to take the traditional arrangement of finance regulated by banking systems and convert it into something that makes everyone gain profit without potentially entering a pool of danger.

Loans and Stable Coins

Another widely used feature of decentralized finance is the loan process which allows you to instantly get your required loan and create a smart contract; but how does it do this? Well, the answer to that is quite simple as the collateral for failing to give back the loan, in this case, is a cryptocurrency that we know has immense value in the stock market.

IF YOU WERE to take a loan through the traditional finance methods, you would essentially have to meet a bank employee who would review your financial situation and set a plan consisting of an interest rate and seize your collateral in case you are unable to pay it back.

THIS WHOLE PROCESS is quite complicated and has its fair share of risks and damages involved, but this is not the case with decentralized finance. Everything that happens within the boundaries of decentralized finance occurs under stable coins, which in other words, are also a form of cryptocurrency that is pegged to the US dollar.

ONE OF THE reasons why stable coins are used with decentralized finance is because their price and value do not change over time, or in other words, they do not fluctuate to a great extent with time. Back in 2014, the first-ever stable coin was created, which is called Tether, and afterward, multiple others came around worldwide.

. . .

BACK BEFORE, decentralized finance was a huge thing, and people heavily relied on the traditional finance method that involved banks, third parties, brokers, etc. the stable coin was used as a way to buy other cryptocurrency tokens such as Bitcoin, but today it can be seen as an intermediate for lending, payments, trading, etc.

Why do Stable Coins Matter?

As mentioned earlier, smart coins were primarily used as a way to purchase other forms of cryptocurrency such as Bitcoins, etc., mainly because all of these cryptocurrencies were not able to be used by traditional banking.

HOWEVER, with the latest advancements and technology, stable coins can be used with decentralized finance on a twenty-four-hour basis, seven days a week, and anywhere around the globe. Besides this, another important feature of stable coins which makes them highly valuable is that they can easily be used with smart contracts on blockchain technology. Earlier in the chapter, we briefly talked about the smart contract but did not get into the details and workings of it all.

IN SIMPLE WORDS, a smart contract is basically a self-executing contract by having a mutual agreement between two parties, and in this case, it would be between a buyer and the seller. The agreements and code distributed and shared are directly contained in the blockchain network, making it fully secure and reliable.

Decentralized Money Market

When it comes to understanding the overall concept of a decentralized money market, it can be said that it is a service that safely connects the borrowers with lenders. Compound is an Ethereum based borrowing and lending dApp, which primarily means that you can easily lend your cryptocurrency with the addition of interest on it.

FOR INSTANCE, let's assume that maybe you need some amount of money to pay the rent or buy groceries, but the only funds you have are cryptocurrencies, and so if that is the case, you can deposit your cryptocurrency collateral and borrow against it. Now what happens is that the compound platform automatically connects the lenders with the borrowers, enforces the terms of the loans, and distributes the interest.

THE PROCESS of earning interest on cryptocurrencies has become extremely popular lately, giving rise to yield farming which is simply a term given to the effort of putting crypto assets to work, while seeking to generate the most returns possible.

IF YOU CAN RECALL, earlier in the book, we discussed the decentralized finance components, which essentially includes an infrastructure, decentralized stable money as well as a decentralized money market.

ANOTHER IMPORTANT ASPECT that covers the components is decentralized insurance. Now, you might be wondering what exactly the need for decentralized insurance is and what importance or safety measure does it include when using the DeFi system?

Decentralized Insurance and Its Uses

Although the overall financial system is a well-maintained and secure one, there is still some level of risks that come with every technology or business. You being an individual, who has invested and saved all these cryptocurrency assets/funds, need a way to ensure that they do not get lost by the system, and for this reason, insurance is needed. The answer to this is a decentralized platform that simply connects people who are willing to pay for insurance with those who are willing to insure them with a premium.

JUST LIKE TRANSACTIONS made without the help of a middle man or well-known company such as a working bank or any other financial institution, the concept of decentralized finance also works in a way without any insurance company and everything that occurs in the overall process is done entirely autonomously.

SO HERE LIES the end of the second chapter of the book! Let's now head over to the third chapter of this book which discusses the different types of decentralization and how you could benefit from each one of them. So without any delay, let's get into it.

TYPES OF DECENTRALIZATION

E arlier chapters in the book talked thoroughly about the concept of decentralized finance and why many people around the world prefer this form of the financial system rather than the traditional kind out there.

WHEN IT COMES to understanding decentralization, there are several different types, and each of them is influenced by the country itself and the potential of growth that could happen. In this chapter, we will be taking a look at the different types of decentralization out there and how you, either as a beginner or someone who has started decentralized finance, could benefit from it.

Market and Political Decentralization

To start off, one of the most important things to know when talking about the overall topic of decentralized finance is political decentralization which, in simple terms, mainly uses the idea and concept of having a significant reduction in the authority of the government of policymaking and contracts.

IT MAY SEEM like a difficult thing to understand, but for instance, let's assume that you are someone who is looking to purchase assets in the form of non-fungible tokens. These are tokens that can be bought, sold, and traded as their values fluctuate over time.

SO INSTEAD OF having involvement from the bank for official paperwork and rights, you can easily purchase them on DeFi and never have to worry about the policies that are regulated by the government. The reason for this is simply because, in DeFi, the workings and control are not operated by the government or any middle man; hence anyone from anywhere can perform it.

MARKET DECENTRALIZATION

THE NEXT TYPE of decentralization is market decentralization which simply uses the idea of privatization and deregulation. You might be wondering what these two terms are, and to put it simply, they are corporations that are accompanied by market development policies and economic liberation.

THE CONCEPT of market decentralization is to allow markets and a large number of local areas with services. Decentralization as a whole can increase national and political stability by allowing its citizens to have control over their financial situation with a system best suited for them.

How different DeFi is being used

Earlier in the book, we talked about a decentralization app called dApps, which simply is a middle way for making simple or complex financial transactions anywhere in the world. There are other forms of programs that are administered through protocols. DApps and protocol both handle simple transactions in the two cryptocurrencies, Bitcoin and Ethereum.

SOME OTHER WAYS decentralization finance is being used is DEX which stands for decentralization exchanges. In the current times, the majority of the cryptocurrency investors out there use popular and reliable exchanges such as Coin-base or Gemini as these services facilitate peer-to-peer transactions. Besides this, it also allows users to retain and control their personal funds and assets.

ANOTHER HIGHLY POPULAR way decentralized finance is being used is by flash loans. In simple words, a flash loan is a form of practical transaction that is done by two main parties, the lender and the borrower. The way this works is when borrowers enter a contract encoded on the Ethereum blockchain to earn money without the help of any lawyer or any third person.

NON-FUNGIBLE TOKEN (NFT)

.   .   .

IF YOU ARE someone who is unaware of non-fungible tokens and how they are used, they are simply considered as limited-time edition digital assets that are acquired by a person through online gaming or exhibitions. The whole concept of non-fungible tokens is that, since they are a form of cryptocurrency tokens, their value can fluctuate depending on the market size and demand.

HENCE BEING the owner of these tokens can help you earn more profit over time. However, the initial stages of getting to own these non-fungible tokens are risky as you have to invest a certain amount of money before you can start earning.

ONE OF THE main reasons why non-fungible tokens are highly valuable is because they are one of a kind, and unlike other items that can be trademarked, shared, etc., these tokens have one owner only, at all times.

WHEN TALKING about non-fungible tokens with decentralized finance, it can be said that they are quite similar, and through DeFi, you can hold, sell, buy and trade these cryptocurrency tokens.

SO FAR IN THE BOOK, we have discussed the most popular cryptocurrency token out there called Bitcoin; however, besides that, these non-fungible tokens, which come in the form of game/art exhibitions assets, are all a way to raise and invest money without acquiring the help from any bank or intermediary person or organization. Since you have complete autonomy over your finances, you can easily keep your tokens in a digital wallet such as Ethereum.

Initial Coin Offerings (ICOs)

Many people out there are well aware of decentralized finance and the use of cryptocurrency but do not realize the value of initial coin offerings and their overall use in the finance sector. When talking about initial coin offerings, they are simply a type of crowdfunding which are mostly and mainly used for raising money for open projects. Now you might be wondering, "what does this have to do with decentralized finance?"

WELL, like we have mentioned multiple times before, DeFi is mainly used as it removes intermediaries such as banks, third-party holders, and other financial institutions, and this is exactly what an initial coin offering does. By having a direct link with the company and investors, you are able to invest and earn profit without acquiring help from any middle man or authority.

NOW WHEN IT comes to initial coin offerings, there are actually two types that are used depending on the level and standard of your interest. Let's take a look at these two ICOs and break their differences down.

PUBLIC INITIAL COIN offering (ICO)

WHEN IT COMES to public initial coin offerings, they are a form of investment that requires the interest and hold of any public figure, meaning that anyone can participate and invest in it to gain some form of profit. If you are someone who has a deep knowledge of finance, marketing, technology, and the law, you can easily take leverage in the decentralized finance of blockchain technology.

PRIVATE INITIAL COIN offering (ICO)

THE MAIN DIFFERENCE between public ICO and private is that in private; only a limited number of investors and other parties can invest and take part in the whole process from the beginning to the end. With private initial coin offering, the majority of the time, only large accredited and high net worth individuals participate.

OVERALL THOUGH, the process of using initial coin offerings to create tokens that would be stored on Ethereum, etc., is also a type of decentralization finance as no third party involvement is required.

Decentralized App (dApp)

You might be wondering what are dApps and how are they used? Well, to answer your question dApps are actually digital platforms/applications or programs that are used and run by blockchain technology. Instead of working on a single computer, these dApps are run by multiple computers, and so they are considered to be peer-to-peer (p2p).

ONE OF THE unique things about dApps is that they are often built on Ethereum and can be used for a variety of purposes ranging from things like gaming and social media to finance. Since these dApps are decentralized, it means that they are free to download and are accessible by any individual without having any sort of connection and interruption from one authority or middle man who has authority.

THERE ARE many benefits to having dApps which we will talk about in detail in the upcoming chapters of the book. For now, though, it is important to know that dApps also provide a way for individuals to create, use and earn profit without having any interruption from a person or corporation who controls and operates the system.

SO HERE LIES the end of the third chapter of the book! It's time that we move on to the next chapter, where we will talk about some factors that influence the growth and rise of a successful decentralization.

4

FACTORS THAT LEAD TO A SUCCESSFUL DECENTRALIZATION

So in the previous chapter of this book, we went through some of the different types of decentralized finance and talked in detail about how you can earn profit through the help of certain forms of cryptocurrency tokens such as non-fungible tokens in games/art as well as two different types of initial coin offering (ICO).

IN THIS CHAPTER of the book, we will be taking a look at some factors that directly or indirectly influence the growth of decentralization. One thing worth mentioning, though, is that decentralization works in such a way that it stores databases and records across many different computers to ensure that it is safe and protected from hackers, etc.

So THE ONE question that you might have thought of by now is how does decentralization finance work, and to what degree can it affect the digital economy of different countries out there? Though the answer to this question is a rather subjective one depending on the level of your interest and knowledge, it can, however, be said that in upcoming years decentralized finance has the potential to completely transform financial intermediation. Let's begin this chapter and talk about some factors that lead to success in the decentralization finance sector as well as the potential gradient of this form of system.

Workings of Initial Coin Offerings (ICOs)

In the previous chapter of the book, we briefly talked about the purpose of initial coin offerings and how these can be used in relation to decentralization finance. When it comes to ICOs, you should know that it is a rather sophisticated and complex process that requires the knowledge and workings of someone who is an expert in areas of finance, marketing, and overall business. Every initial coin offering starts with the business's intention to raise capital which will further be used in secondary stages of finances. The company's people will begin by creating a campaign and work to raise the overall capital. After that's done, the next step is to create a token that will be used to represent an asset or utility in the blockchain market.

THE CREATION of these tokens is a relatively easy process as you are not creating a code for an entirely new cryptocurrency but rather using the already existing cryptocurrency and slightly modifying it. During this stage, the company will usually try to lure in investors to promote their campaign, and while this is being done, the investors can expect to use the acquired tokens created by the company or wait until the value increases. Overall though, the creation and phenomenon of an initial coin offering is a relatively new idea in the finance sector, and so combining it with the concept and rules of decentralization finance can be performed to achieve success.

Important dApps to Know for Growth

As we have mentioned earlier, there are dApps that are run on a blockchain network of computers instead of relying on a single computer that is administered and controlled by a single authority. Although there are multiple applications out there that are used for free to increase the flexibility of development, reduce censorship, etc.

ONE OF THE most common apps out there is called the UniSwap, which has been able to facilitate more than $1 billion. Besides this app, an app called AAVE can also be used, which allows users to lend and borrow cryptocurrency tokens.

OVERALL THOUGH, the prime reason that dApps are beginning to take over the traditional forms of app out there is that they are more trusted by users since the users themselves get the control and ownership of their personal assets and overall data. Now you might be asking yourself, "what sort of information or data is stored in dApps and how does it help to fully secure it?"

WELL, the answer to that is that dApps mainly use the wallet address of users where digital assets and funds are located. Besides this, interactions that are made in the digital world, such as uploaded posts, trading, loans, etc., are all located on the blockchain on which the app is supported.

Smart Contracts

One of the things that are operated with decentralized finance are smart contracts which are essentially an area where code is stored on any blockchain platform. Just like decentralized finance, there is absolutely no need for an intermediate to come in and handle the workings of smart contracts.

THE REASON why this is important is that once the smart contract is deployed, they become immutable, and the transactions made after will be recorded and stored on the blockchain for everyone to openly view. For instance, let's assume that a smart contract is operated to perform and handle the currency exchanges between two parties. So, in this case, if the smart contract is able to successfully verify the currency from each of the two parties, then it will safely execute the transaction without requiring help and interference from a third party such as a banker.

ONE UNIQUE THING that makes smart contracts stand out is that they are able to facilitate a different number of operations, and most of the time, an application of dApp will rely on multiple smart contracts which are all linked together.

SO TO CONCLUDE, this shows that smart contracts are a way for you to make transactions such as lending, borrowing, etc., in a transparent, secure, and efficient manner. Without the involvement of a middle man like the traditional finance system, you are able to easily and securely make transactions without the requirement of physical paperwork.

Potential Growth for DeFi

Although the decentralized finance system has been around for a short period of time, one thing that is prominent is its power to completely change and transform the already present traditional system. There is a vast growth potential for DeFi mainly because it uses the concept of not relying on one corporation for authority but rather gives equal opportunity to every individual.

FOR INSTANCE, in decentralized finance, the option to exchange digital assets like Bitcoin to another digital asset in the marketplace can be seen as a way for you to earn profit. The removal of steps that normally would be used by a bank or any financial system and replacing it with a secure blockchain account not only makes it more reliable but also efficient.

MOREOVER, another factor that influences the growth of decentralized finance is the ability to lend, borrow and save through smart contracts. This not only eliminates the need to make official paperwork and pay for services that you typically get from any institution, but it also makes it completely transparent.

OVERALL THOUGH, it can be said that decentralized finance empowers individuals to have a sense of control over their assets more than traditional finance. With the option to allow an individual to choose their own assets and investments, this could make the future of handling financial systems completely different than the current one.

BESIDES THAT, another great thing about decentralization finance is that it is able to step into the world of business-to-business interaction by having smart contracts and tokenization, which could be used with dApps.

. . .

So, at last, we have come to the end of the fourth chapter of the book as well. Hopefully, by the end of this, you were able to take away some knowledge regarding the scope of decentralization finance. It's time now that we head over to the next chapter of the book, which talks in great depth about how decentralized finance works.

5

HOW DOES DECENTRALIZED FINANCE WORK?

So just to recap all of the things that we learned and talked about in the previous chapter regarding decentralized finance, it is simply a form of a system by which financial products become accessible to individuals who wish to own them through borrowing, lending, etc. without the help from any middle man such as a bank or any other financial institution.

WHEN WE TAKE a look at our current financial system, we get to understand that everything that happens, whether it be you taking a loan, managing saving funds, insurance, and much more, is all controlled by an authoritative figure. The person or any organization such as a government who controls your financial matters in return has a set of rules that you have to abide by in order to get your work done.

AS WE KNOW that financial systems are not at all similar in all of the countries around the world. There are restrictions, laws, guides, processes, and much more complicated stuff that you have to go through in order to get access to your financial matters.

So by now, if you haven't guessed already, all of these processes or steps require not only time and a tremendous amount of effort but also a service fee which you have to pay in order to regulate and keep money flowing in your own economy.

Keeping all of this in mind, when we introduce decentralized finance into our system, it means that we are allowing ourselves to be free from all the hassle and bustle that we would have to experience had we continued with our current system. In this chapter, we will be taking a look at how decentralized finance really works and what sort of pros and cons you could gain from it, so without any further delay, let's get into it.

Peer to Peer Dealings / Work

So we know that the whole concept of decentralized finance works and refers to the system by which software written on the blockchain is used to empower seller, buyer, and lender to come together and interact with each other, and by doing so, they are eliminating the interruption of any bank or public figure who controls and manages finances.

Knowing this, you can probably imagine by now that several of the latest technologies and sets of protocols are used to achieve the overall goal of decentralization. Although, all of this may sound quite intriguing and can be seen as a way for the world to move towards higher advancement, the question that arises in the mind and hearts of many when they get to know about decentralized finance is; why is it important and why was this concept not applied a long time ago?

IN THE PRESENT WORLD, we know that the use and regulation of financial services is not something new, and the majority of the population, regardless of background, have some sort of knowledge regarding it. Today we can clearly see that the majority of the transactions and dealings are done regularly through online banking/institutions that have combined the latest technology with advertisements.

HOWEVER, it must be noted that the involvement of technology is just limited to a certain amount, mainly up to facilitating transactions. This is where the decentralization finance workings come into place to counteract the effects a country faces, such as jurisdiction laws, different standards and beliefs, competitions in the finance market, and the overall economy and business level.

Decentralized Exchanges

One common thing that many individuals are currently performing with the help of decentralized finance is transactions of money like borrowing and supplying in order to earn some degree of interest. The key thing to know about taking out a loan or borrowing money In decentralized finance is that it is not the same as getting a loan from your bank, where you essentially bring future cash flows forward for inspection of the bank, so that the bank may determine whether or not you are worthy of a loan.

. . .

LOANS within decentralized finance are more like getting a loan from your local pawnbroker. Now in case you are someone who does not know how this works, customers can take an item like a particular car, musical instrument, piece of jewelry, or really any item of value to the pawnbrokers and receive a loan based on the value of the item. The pawnbroker might lend you 50% of the value of the item, then accordingly charge you interest, and if you miss your repayments, they might sell your item to recoup the value of the loan. Pawnbrokers will always lend you less than the value of the item you're putting up for collateral, and this is known as an over collateralized loan.

BORROWING in Decentralized finance can be considered quite similar to the scenario explained above. So in order to get a loan, you need to initially bring collateral, and in this case, a cryptocurrency that is essentially locked up in a smart contract called a collateralized debt position or SDP in short.

One important thing worth mentioning, though, is that if you are borrowing money in decentralized finance, it will be over collateralized, and if the value of the collateral falls to a great extent, you can potentially have your crypto liquidated by the SDP to cover the loan. You can consider it like pawnbrokers selling an item to cover a loan that has failed.

The Working Process of Decentralization Finance (DeFi-system)

So in order to get started with decentralized finance, it is crucial to understand that this system's blockchain uses keys to ensure that the data and other private information are secured. By using this form of technology, you are able to get access to a unique key that will be used for identification purposes.

. . .

GENERALLY, though, you will get two forms of keys, one public and the other being private, and this overall process is called asymmetric cryptography. Now you might be wondering what exactly the need for a key is when there is blockchain technology to store databases.

Well, the reason why the public "key" system is used is for your peers to locate and reach you on the overall system itself. On the other hand, the private key is mainly used to get access to the transactions that you will make as well as perform certain actions on the DeFi blockchain platform.

Transactions

ONE THING WORTH MENTIONING, though, is that since cryptocurrency is involved in this system, your private key is primarily also used to buy, sell and even trade the cryptocurrency. You might be wondering how transactions are made? The answer to that is quite simple in order to send a transaction to any of your peers; you need a private key.

ONCE YOU DO SO, your system will easily be able to create a block representing that particular transaction and quickly notify the system itself for verification purposes. After all of this has been done, the system and others will verify it, and if it goes through as a valid request, then it will add the block to the ledger.

MANY PEOPLE HAVE issues regarding the safety of the system itself, but this has been covered as you can get a pseudo-anonymous address. The benefit of having and owning is that no one can see the name but only the address.

Elements of the DeFi Ecosystem

WHEN IT COMES to decentralization finance networks, there are certain elements that make up the overall ecosystem. Earlier in the book, we went through stable coins and smart contracts; however, these only make up one part of the entire ecosystem, and in reality, there are other elements attached to it.

ONE IMPORTANT THING TO understand when it comes to DeFi is open ledger standards which are used by the majority of the companies. The main reason these are used by companies is to ensure complete interoperability. Now the question that stands out is what would happen if open ledger standards were not used?

TO ANSWER THE QUESTION, without open ledger standards, the applications of decentralization would not be compatible with each other. Other benefits of this include complete transparency, immutability, permission-less network, and, lastly, faster transaction.

SO THAT IS all for this chapter, folks! It is time that we head over to the next chapter of this book which shines a light on the main differences between open finance and decentralization finance. So without any further delay, let's get right into it.

6

OPEN FINANCE VS. DECENTRALIZED FINANCE (DEFI)

S o far in the book, we have thoroughly talked about the purpose of decentralized finance and what are some of the elements that truly make up the ecosystem. One thing that is clear about whether we are talking about decentralized finance or open finance is that all of it requires some form of order either from an authority or from within the system.

BEFORE THE COVID 19 had an impact on the world, everyone used to live in a balanced manner where people followed the rules and regulations set by an upper authority such as the government, but as the world saw a dramatic shift, the economic and financial world changed.

HIGHER UPPER-CLASS BUSINESSES/ORGANIZATIONS started to deviate from the traditional system to create an entirely new system where people had more say in their matters than any figure or authority in power.

. . .

NOW YOU MIGHT BE WONDERING what the main differences are between open finance and decentralized finance and what pros and cons do these systems hold. In this chapter, we will be taking a look at these two systems and comparing them side by side to help you get a clear understanding of both. So without any more delay, let's get into it.

What Exactly is Open Finance

Now when the majority of the people hear the term open finance, they might think it is simply another word for open banking, which then leads them to believe that it is a system of place where individuals of a country could share their financial assets/funds.

HOWEVER, it is slightly different as in open finance; there is a data-sharing model which allows individuals of all ages and backgrounds to share not only their financial data but other forms as well.

NOW YOU MIGHT HAVE STRUCK the question of how is open finance different to open banking. Well, the answer to that is that in open finance, users have the opportunity to share their banking information with other potential workers such as people working in firms/companies/etc. with the help of a third party interference such as API (Application Programming Interfaces).

. . .

ONE OF THE great things about open finance is that it opens doors to other potential benefits, such as including data from insurances, fiscal authorities, pension funds, and even utility provider companies to build new models with the help of the past model.

IT IS worth mentioning that in open finance, there is a use of blockchain technology by Fintech (financial technology) companies in addition to API integration. The reasons behind this are to improve data transparency and give the consumers a way to make better financial decisions.

Growth of Financial Technology

Back in 2020, for the average human being with normal living standards only 2.5% of the apps on their phone were dedicated to online banking and finances but as time went on, this part of the industry saw a massive, exponential growth; which in turn gave people around the world a platform to safely access and use financial management tools.

THIS, in turn, had a positive effect on traditional banking systems as they allowed their customers to access new products, expanding the growth overall. Now, although this allowed consumers of all backgrounds to have a better say in how their financial assets are being used, it still comes from the roots of the traditional financial system as there is an authority that controls and regulates these financial matters.

ON THE OTHER HAND, decentralized finance uses this idea and completely turns it by eliminating the need for financial institutions to have a say and instead gives consumers powerful and effective automation-driven blockchain-based financial services. Now while keeping these two in mind, it can be said that the world of finance and its systems are changing rapidly, but while this is a form of advancement, we have to think about the consumers and how directly it is impacting them.

WITH THE RISE OF COMPETITION, it could be a challenge for individuals to differentiate open finance and decentralized finance, although they both hold two fundamentally different concepts.

API's and Functions

If you are someone who has little to no idea of what Application programming interfaces are, they are simply a set of codes that have protocols that are used to determine how well different forms of software can communicate and share information with each other.

KEEPING THAT IN MIND, the application programming interface is used with open finance to safely facilitate the sharing of important data between banks and third parties related to it. Now while open finance has an infrastructure of its own without being controlled by government regulations, the overall operation is still considered a traditional finance system as the banks and third parties related are all subject to government order and regulations.

NOW YOU MIGHT BE WONDERING that although this system relies on the already present traditional system, what are some of the key benefits it provides to the consumer and the economy. Well, in simple words, the overall concept of open finance is to help individuals by assisting them. With the help of existing and new API, everything becomes simpler, and so time spent is reduced.

BESIDES THIS, a benefit this has on the economy is that banks are able to once again operate and have full control regarding legal matters such as loans, transfers, and financing. Although everything is performed and regulated on a single administration, there are without a doubt certain drawbacks that also need to be considered.

Flaws of Open Finance

Although the system of open finance is directly linked to the already present traditional finance that involves the intermediary of banking and other financial institutions, there are, however, a few disadvantages that need to be highlighted when comparing it with decentralized finance. One of the common things about open finance is that it is an ecosystem that comes with multiple stakeholders, which includes and is not limited to regulators, government, consumers, third-party providers as well as data providers. Since there are lots of parties, application programming interfaces are used to maintain connections, it is highly possible that friction of some sort occurs between parties in the form of disagreements, mismanagement, etc.

BESIDES THIS, one other issue with open finance that directly needs to be taken off is its security issue. Although the overall is built upon premium security and can be reliable, it can only do so to an extent.

. . .

As we all know, in open finance, consumer data is shared amongst different levels of parties/institutions, and this could provide a great opportunity for hackers to initiate attacks by stealing the data. Hence it can be quite costly to maintain a level of security with the highly advanced technology system that open finance uses.

Now, this might seem like a serious issue, and while it is, it is also important to look on the bright side of it all. Which is that every system contains some degree of sensitivity that can lead to a loss. So it is important that strict measures are taken against them to prevent corruption and mismanagement.

Future of the Finance System

Whether it be open finance where consumers are able to give their data to a higher authority or whether it be decentralized finance, one thing that every one of us can agree upon is the challenges that these systems will face. While they are on the brink of reaching utmost success due to highly competitive technology and system development, there are risks associated.

Keeping that in mind, it can be said that the use of blockchain technology in decentralized finance is a rather better approach as it is not only transparent but also gives individuals more control of their own finances. The addition of smart contracts to make easy and efficient transactions is a way to empower and gain the trust of the consumers who are shifting into this new paradigm.

. . .

So, in a nutshell, we can safely say that with open finance, users are able to experience a financial system that is more convenient and on the other hand, decentralized finance uses the concept of digital assets and developing financial products, which could set as a pavement for individuals to earn more profit.

WITH THE RISE and popularity of this new financial system, it is apparent that the world of banking is coming to an end and that powerful financial products in digital form are beginning to increase in value.

SO HERE LIES the end of the sixth chapter of the book! It is time that we shift to the next chapter of the book, which will all be about the systems in decentralized finance and how you could start familiarizing yourself with them.

7

WHAT IS DECENTRALIZATION AND THE SYSTEMS IN DEFI

After reading the last chapter of the book, which talked all about the two financial systems, open finance and decentralized finance, you probably have been able to distinguish between the two and understand in detail the purpose of these two systems. However, in this chapter, we will be merely focusing on decentralization finance again and have a look at the systems involved in DeFi, which makes it efficient and smart.

So far in the book, we have learned about decentralized finance, which is related to cryptocurrency. So, for instance, you could purchase any cryptocurrency such as Bitcoin or in other forms such as non-fungible tokens (NFT), which can be stored on a digital wallet such as Ethereum.

The great thing about storing assets and funds on the digital wallet is that it stays with you forever, even after the place or game where you initially bought or traded it from has been demolished. These assets that are in the form of coins or objects can increase in value over time, and if you choose to trade them, the data of the transaction will be stored on blockchain technology, thus proving its convenience and reliability.

IN THIS CHAPTER, however, we will be taking a look at if decentralized finance can work without cryptocurrency and what are the four different types of stable coins. So without further ado, let's start.

101 of Decentralized Finance

So throughout this entire book, you have probably understood that in decentralized finance, you are able to access your digital assets, share, lend, and buy them according to your liking without the need of a middle man or financial support group.

THE REASON behind its popularity and sudden growth from 2018, when it was first released, has a lot to do with the fact that it is efficient, fast, and more secure than using traditional finance methods.

WHEN LOOKING at the current system, it is not that you are not able to get any benefits or anything; the reason why people have shifted their interest is because of the time and effort that goes in. On the other hand, a decentralized financial system, which is mainly based on blockchain technology, gives every individual the opportunity to have authority rather than relying on others to manage your finance.

. . .

By now, you probably are wondering about the peer-to-peer inter system that is linked heavily with decentralized finance. To clear that, let's take for an example a compound which is an example of a peer to peer decentralized lending platform that allows you to interact with your fellow peers in a more efficient and fast manner, as opposed to taking help from an official authority such as a bank to do your work.

Besides this, another important thing regarding decentralized finance is that it is non-custodial, which basically means that consumers like you are able to gain full control and access to your funds, assets, and all sorts of data. When you make a transaction, the data is stored on blockchain technology, and everyone is able to view it, but no one can steal, modify, or corrupt that information/funds.

Four Kinds of Stable Coins

One of the key elements of decentralized finance is the use of stable coins, as they are much better and more efficient than cryptocurrency tokens. Why, you may ask? Well, the reason for this is quite simple as with cryptocurrency, they are usually more volatile, and when used in the overall system of DeFi, it can imbalance the nature and system of it all.

On the other hand, stable coins are usually linked with real-life world money such as the US dollar. When you or anyone owns a stable coin that has a value of 1 dollar or any other USD, its value does not change or fluctuate over time like the way cryptocurrency value does. Let's take a look in-depth at the four main types of stable coins and what their function and purpose are in decentralized finance.

Crypto Collateralized

Before we begin talking about crypto collateralized, let's break it down by first understanding what the term collateralized means and how does it apply to the world of decentralized finance. In simple words, collateralized means that a borrower owns property or an asset that will be taken away and given to the lender if the borrower fails to pay back the loan.

THE OVERALL USE is to ensure that the loan is attached with an asset that is valuable, hence completely securing it. Now coming to the topic of crypto collateralized, it is extremely valuable and of use, as it allows for the dynamic maintenance of consistent and balanced market price. On a dynamic level, it means to provide a sort of buffer against the rising and falling of price.

NOW YOU MIGHT BE WONDERING how you could obtain collateralized crypto tokens? So in order to do that, you would have to completely secure your collateral tokens into a smart contract, so this way, you can easily retrieve them later by paying stable coins in the smart contract. Some of the most common and well-used crypto collateralized tokens are the Maker DAO (DAI) and EOSDT Token.

Fiat Collateralized

If you are someone who has never heard of this term before, then there is absolutely nothing to worry about because, as the name suggests, it is a type of stable coin which is backed by real-life sovereign currency such as the dollar or the pound. Now in order to obtain this form of stable coins, you would essentially have to offer a dollar form of reserves which are equivalent to the value of the stable coin.

ONE OF THE great things about fiat collateralized is that besides using real-life cash that can be translated into the exact value of these stable coins, you can also use gold. Besides this, fiat collateralized stable coins are often pegged as a 1:1 ratio, which is not the case with crypto collateralized stable coins.

LET'S ASSUME, for the purpose of understanding fiat collateralized stable coins, that you are someone who wants to take out/redeem cash for your coins. So what would happen is that the entity or the system that manages your stable coins, the digital wallet, will take it out and, in return, will take the real cash value that you have stored. The amount taken will be equivalent to the value of the coin and will be sent to your bank account. So, in the end, the equivalent stable coins are either burned or completely removed from the system. Some of the most common and used stable coins for fiat collateralize are the Pax dollar, Gemini dollar, XSGD, and Statis EURS token.

Commodity Collateralized Stable Coins.

When it comes to talking about commodity collateralized stable coins, they are quite different from the previous two as in this case, it is a type of stable coin which uses commodities such as gold or silver. Although these two are most commonly used, many people prefer platinum, oil, and even other precious and rare metals.

.   .   .

THIS ESSENTIALLY MEANS that you are able to hold a real-life asset that is equivalent in value to the stable coin overall. Since real-life assets are used in relation to stable coins, many people choose to keep these stable coins as it has the potential to increase in value over time.

FOR INSTANCE, the Digix Gold (DGX) is an ERC token that is primarily built on the Ethereum network, as we talked about before. This form of a digital asset is actually backed up by real-life value that is one gram of physical gold. This real physical gold is only stored in Singapore, and many people/owners of the digix gold tend to redeem these stable coins in return for the actual physical gold. Since gold can be considered a strong asset due to its ever-growing demand and value, it is used with this stable coin.

Non-Collateralized

Lastly, the fourth type of stable coin is the non-collateralized, which has no chain of real-life physical or other forms of assets linked to it. The mechanism of this form of stable coin works by people believing and holding on to its existing value.

NOW YOU MIGHT BE THINKING, where did the overall idea come to create a non-collateralized stable coin? The answer to that is the US dollar which was once backed up by gold. This form of the stable coin uses the seignorage shares, which is essentially an algorithmically governed approach. When keeping the previous three stable coins in mind, this form of stable coin is the most decentralized out of the four as it is not collateralized to any other asset, whether it be digital or a real-life one.

. . .

THE TRICKY THING and perhaps the challenging part of non-collateralized stable coins is that they require continuous growth in order to stay in the market, and once their value and demand have decreased significantly, other forms of the stable coin will lead, and no other collateral could liquidate the coin back into its form. Some important non-collateralized stable coins in the market at the current time are the Terra and AMPL.

SO THIS CONCLUDES the seventh chapter of the book! It is now time to flip and head over to the eighth chapter of the book, which mainly talks about all the advantages that come with decentralized finance.

ADVANTAGES OF DECENTRALIZATION NETWORKS

I n our day-to-day lives, we all are consumed by one thing or another, whether it be the responsibility of work or family. At times it can become quite difficult to manage all these things and at the same time work to provide for your family and unfortunately with the rise of Covid 19 back in 2020, the world saw a dramatic shift in not only its individual economy but also in the financial sector as hundreds of thousands of people either had to leave their job or were expelled.

ALTHOUGH THESE ARE CONSIDERED as bad rough times for the majority of the population, there was, however, a rise in advancement that was made not only in the physical world but also in the electronic digital world. The world we live in today is completely different from that of 100 years ago as there are new systems, rules and regulations, technology, and so much more that push every individual to strive towards greater things.

. . .

WHILE STAYING on the topic of decentralized finance, it can be said that it has been able to completely revamp the traditional system of finance by removing the need for complex processes handled by companies/firms and organizations in the finance area. In this chapter, we will be taking a look at some of the major pros that have transformed the digital world with the help of decentralized finance. So without any delay, continue on reading.

Immutability

To start off, the reason why decentralized finance has reached a successful peak is mainly because of its effective utilization of cryptocurrency in a safe and effective manner. Besides this, the help gained from the consensus algorithm truly helps this overall platform to work with blockchain to achieve complete immutability.

NOW YOU MIGHT BE WONDERING what sort of pros does immutability provide? Well, the good thing about it is that with the help of immutability, no one is able to manipulate, steal or modify any sort of data as it is stored on the blockchain technology, making it transparent and secure. With everyone's data, there is a name and information attached to it, which everyone is able to see.

SO OVERALL, it can be said that with immutability, the overall decentralized finance platform is able to be more secure and reliable. All sorts of financial/asset transactions made in decentralized finance can easily be done with complete security and transparency.

· · ·

DUE TO THE rise of financial crisis in different countries of the world, people started doubting the overall concept and integrity of the traditional system. So with the help of digital assets that are stored and have the same value as real-life cash/gold/silver, you are easily able to make transactions without the worry of high inflation, government policies and regulations and much more.

Games and Lotteries

Throughout the course of this book, we were able to shine a light on the elements and aspects of decentralized finance, which makes it reliable and more secure. However, one of the major things that many people around the world use decentralized finance is for gaming. Now you might be wondering, "how does that work and why is it counted as an advantage?"

WELL, to answer your question, with the help of decentralized finance, participants are able to come together and play no-loss games. By putting in a digital value in the game, users can play and earn profit without having losses, as after the game ends, individuals will get their money back. The system through which this works is by smart contracts, which are made on blockchain technology and are used to create these games.

Lending - Borrowing System

Another major advantage that comes with decentralizing finance is the development of peer-to-peer lending and borrowing, which allows every individual to get a loan without having to go through the traditional process of paperwork, licensing, etc.

. . .

BESIDES THIS, the addition of smart contracts completely ensures that there is absolutely zero interference from third parties like brokers, bankers, and financial advisers/experts. Since decentralized finance production back in mid-2018, the world has seen great progress through applications of DeFi, which are completely safe and secure; so that your financial matters are stored in a transparent, yet safe way.

ALTHOUGH THERE ARE many DeFi lending and borrowing platforms out there, one of the most commonly used ones is the Compound which is an application that allows the lender to give cryptocurrency assets like Non-fungible tokens/Bitcoin, etc. to a specific number of the lending pool.

YOU COULD THINK of it as a way for lenders to earn profit as they lend their assets to a borrower; they can easily charge an interest rate that will help them earn profit. Some people are hesitant towards personal lending assets in the form of stable coins and cryptocurrency tokens, but since every transaction, whether it be purchasing or lending, is made and stored entirely as a data block on blockchain technology, users have nothing to worry about.

IF YOU ARE someone who is looking to lend your digital assets to any borrower to earn maximum profit, you should keep in mind that the profit you earn is dependent on how much contribution you make to the borrowing pool; thus, the more you lend, the more profit you earn.

System of Tokenization

When talking about the topic of the benefits of decentralized finance, it is crucial to talk about tokenization as it plays a major role in this system. Earlier in the book, we have mentioned how crypto tokens are essentially digital tokens that are present on the blockchain and carry a great value in terms of how you choose to spend it. Although there are countless tokens out there, some of the most notable and important ones include security tokens, utility tokens, and real estate tokens.

Now while we know tokens are essential, how can we maximize their use for our own profit? The answer to that is quite simple and forward as these tokens can be used to help you get different functionalities. For instance, with the help of these tokens, you are able to achieve a percentage of real physical property or land that otherwise would not be possible.

Security tokens can primarily be used as digital assets in any specific application on the digital market. Not only that, tokens like the ones we have discussed could help you open a way to get other digital/physical assets such as fiat currencies, digital currencies, silver, and even gold. These tokens and other assets are stored on an Ethereum based system in the form of collateralized coins.

Savings

The introduction of decentralized finance in this part of the sector has opened a way for people to comfortably manage their financial assets/funds without having to disclose personal information to bankers or any person working in the finance field. As we have mentioned earlier in the book, the opportunity for people to lock their crypto assets into lending platforms like compound, they can eventually earn a set of profit in the form of interest.

THIS INTEREST HOLDS great value and can be used as a way to earn and save money. Let's assume you are someone who wants to keep your bank open while lending your crypto assets to a borrower. Now what will happen is that as long as you lend the asset, you have the power to demand and gain interest from it, which you could deposit and save in your bank.

ALTHOUGH THIS FORM of managing personal finance relies on the traditional finance system, many people have started to move away and focus more on decentralized finance saving applications. There is a term that has widely been known to people called yield farming which is essentially a practice for users to move their valuable cryptocurrency assets in different lending protocols to earn maximum profit. As of today, there are many applications of DeFi savings out there, and the most common and widely used ones are Argent, pool together, and dharma.

No Service / Creditable Fees

The last advantage that we will be discussing is regarding the use of services and how you can use decentralized finance without having to pay fees. Before we get into that, let's talk about why there is a need to pay fees in centralized finance. The reason why this is necessary is that a major portion of your private finance/information is being handled by a third party; hence it is centralized. This essentially means that it involves the government's rules and regulations, and so in order to keep a country stable in terms of its economy, it is essential for money to flow from one party to another.

ON THE OTHER HAND, decentralized finance used this system and completely revamped it to completely diminish the need for service fees as you as an individual have complete autonomy over your personal financial matters. By having a secure system of smart contracts on an Ethereum based network, users easily and efficiently manage their funds/assets.

AND WITH THAT BEING SAID, we have come to the end of this chapter as well, folks! Although there are countless other benefits related to decentralized finance, you now know about a few major ones. Let's continue reading this book and head over to the next chapter, which guides on how you can invest in the DeFi platform...

HOW TO INVEST IN DECENTRALIZED FINANCE

I n recent times, the world has seen a dramatic change in the systems of finance and how they are controlled by a central authority such as a bank or a government. Throughout the course of this entire book, you have learned multiple times about the purpose of decentralized finance and how it could help you make secure and efficient transactions without the need for any third person or party.

So since that is out of the way, the question that remains is how can you, as an individual who has little to no guidance or background related to the field of finance could, invest and make a profit off of it. Well, the answer to that is quite an easy one that only requires multiple steps that you have to take care of.

One thing worth mentioning before we get started with the steps to invest in decentralized finance is that in order to earn maximum profit, you have to keep in mind that everything takes time.

YOU WILL NOT BE able to see your profit flourish overnight as there are certain time requirements and information that you need to provide, which obviously needs authentication and verification. So with that out of the way, let's get started on how you can efficiently get into the world of decentralized finance and eliminate the need for any third party handling your personal finances.

Preparing a Secure Wallet

One thing that you have to keep in mind, regardless of whether you have crypto tokens or any other form of a digital or physical asset, is where you will store it, and this factor could influence another secondary working. You might be wondering what exactly the need for a digital wallet is? Well, the reason why you need a digital wallet is so that all your assets or tokens could be in one place rather than scattered in different systems.

THINK of it as a personal home where you have all your bought items stored. For instance, let's assume that you are someone who has earned non-fungible tokens through playing crypto games such as decentral and or axie infinity. Now the asset that you have earned in the form of items in the game holds a value, and although you could store them in the game's own wallet, it is much better to transfer them to a wallet so that in case the game gets demolished, you already have all of your assets secured.

. . .

THERE ARE multiple other examples that you could use, such as storing funds, gold, silver, and other forms of assets. In today's world, there are hundreds of marketplaces where you could store your digital assets, but some of the most popular and secure ones are meta mask, coin base wallets, argent, Ethereum, trust wallet, burner wallet, Gnosis, Fortmatic, my crypto, my ether wallet, wallet connect, torus, and portis.

ONE OF THE key features of having a secure digital wallet is that it's non-custodial, meaning that users can safely transfer or recieve funds, with the knowledge that they are the only entity that has complete access and autonomy. Besides this, wallets are completely accessible, which means that you can handle a suit of assets by using the deposit on which the wallet is based.

Purchasing of Crypto Coins

After you have successfully completed the process of registering for a digital wallet and have verified it, the next most important step is to purchase crypto tokens; although this may seem like a relatively easy step, you should know that in order to have a strong connection in the world of cryptocurrency, you need to do all the proper research.

ONE OF THE most common mistakes people make when it comes to purchasing crypto coins is that they quickly search up the current value of the coin, and without any hesitation, they purchase it from the marketplace and store it in their wallets.

THE THING that they do not realize is that the value of crypto tokens fluctuate on a daily basis, and so in order to be in the safe and profitable pool, it is best that besides researching the value, try doing backup research on its pros, cons, history, the original creator and the potential future benefits.

IF YOU ARE someone who has little to no background in the world of cryptocurrency, it would be recommended that you start with the Ethereum platform, as the majority of the protocols are built over there. Purchasing ether or ERC – 20 coins is a good and safe option when starting with investments. Some other coins that you could purchase are Bitcoin, Solana (SOL), Avalanche (AVAX), polygon, dogecoin, yearn finance, lucky block, Shiba Inu, and Maker.

Getting into Protocols

So let's assume that you have successfully bought crypto tokens and have transferred them to a secure digital wallet, so what is next? Well, the next step when it comes to investing in the world of decentralized finance is to familiarize yourself with protocols and how they work. As we have mentioned earlier in the book, there are protocols out there that allow every user to lend, borrow, trade, and lock up crypto tokens with other users.

INVESTING in a pool can be a great start to earning a maximum profit when other individuals work and trade within the pool, thus helping you save money. The whole purpose and idea behind protocols are to allow lenders and other investors to use your crypto tokens or any other digital/ physical assets, either collateral or non-collateral, and in return, you get to charge an interest rate on it.

. . .

THIS FORM of earning through lending/ borrowing is called yield farming, as we discussed before, and it could be a great start for you to earn profit based on your current digital assets.

IN ORDER TO GET STARTED, you could simply visit the protocol's website and, from there, connect your wallet so that they are safely able to access your assets, and from there, plans will be devised on trading, lending, borrowing, etc.

Tracking your Investments in DeFi

Now that you have stepped into the world of decentralized finance by building a base through crypto tokens, it is important that you keep track of all sorts of transactions that are being made. The reason why you might want to do this is that you, as an individual, are the owner and caretaker of your assets. Since there is no involvement of any third party/middle man like manager/or financial institutions to keep track and regulate your financial assets, it is your job to do so. There are many platforms/applications from where you can track all sorts of activities in decentralized finance, but the most popular one amongst that is Kubera.

IF YOU ARE new to the whole concept of Kubera and want to know how to get started, you could simply start by visiting the website of Kubera, and once you are there, you can click on the sign-up option where your account will be created. Once that is done, the next step is to simply connect your financial account with it. Since Kubera works and integrates with hundreds of banks and all sorts of financial institutions, you can rely on this platform. After you have gone through this step, you can easily continue by adding your data of crypto coins.

.   .   .

SO THESE ARE ALL the steps involved when it comes to investing in the world of decentralized finance. Hopefully, by now, you have a better idea/ understanding of what needs to be done to get started successfully. Let's head over to the tenth chapter of the book, where you will get to know about some DeFi platforms and learn in detail on how you can create a digital wallet.

DEFI PLATFORMS FOR INVESTMENT

I n the previous chapter of this book, we talked in-depth about how you as an individual can start investing in the world of decentralized finance. One thing that we mentioned was the need to create a digital wallet where you are able to store your crypto tokens and other assets such as gold, silver, and stable coins.

HOWEVER, in this chapter, besides talking about some DeFi platforms where you can invest your time and money, we will also be giving you a step to step guide on how you can create a digital wallet.

ONE THING IS CLEAR, though, whether you are starting new into decentralized finance or are someone who has been gaining profit from decentralized finance is that it is relatively new and evolving. Now this means that although these apps and other decentralized finance coins are powerful and hold a value, there is also an equal chance of having a loss.

. . .

ALTHOUGH THIS IS something to keep in mind, the world has seen an astounding amount of growth from this system of finance, and as more people around the world get more involved in it, the likelihood of decentralized finance failing is extremely low. So with that being in mind, let's talk about how you can create a digital wallet where you are able to store your assets.

Hosted Wallets vs. Self-Controlled Wallets

Before we dive into the topic of the different kinds of decentralized finance apps that are available out there in the market, let's first take a look at the two distinct types of wallets that are used and their purpose. In hosted wallets, your crypto coins/stable coins information will be stored and reviewed by a third party. So, for instance, let's assume that you decide to purchase a number of coins off of an application like coin base. Once you do this, your crypto will automatically be held in the hosted wallets, where all the information and background checks will be run and controlled by a third party, similar to how a central bank manages all your finances. One of the key benefits of having this type of wallet is that in case you lose accessing information, you will not lose crypto tokens. While that may seem like a good idea, one drawback to it is that you are not able to get complete access to the crypto coin.

CONTROLLED wallets are often called by another name of non-custodial wallet as in this type of wallet, you are the owner of it, and there is absolutely no involvement of any third party/custodian. Some of the most common and popular self-controlled wallets are Meta masks and coin base wallets, where you can keep your crypto assets safe and secure.

ONE THING WORTH MENTIONING, though, is that in this type of wallet, it is your responsibility to remember the access login information like password, etc., because in case you fail to remember and lose it, you will not be able to access it. Moreover, you should also remember that in non-custodial wallets, if someone gets your personal information, they will get full access to all the assets in there.

HOWEVER, on the bright side, with non-custodial wallets, you have a wide range of secondary access to crypto tokens such as yield farming, lending, borrowing, staking, and so much more.

Setting Up a Wallet (Step-by-Step)

Now that the types of wallets and their use is out of the way let's focus on how you can set up a digital wallet and talk more about the personal information required to access it. After you have successfully done your research regarding which wallet you are going to use for the storage of your assets, the next thing would be to download the software on which the wallet depends.

ONCE THAT IS out of the way, you might want to check the terms and conditions which are associated with the wallet app so that you know what you are getting yourself into. After the app is installed electronically on your device like a phone or a working laptop, you will be asked to create a 12-word private key which only you should know about so you can get access.

. . .

ANOTHER THING that some digital wallet apps requires is bank/cards information and the reason why you need to provide this payment is so that in the future, you have physical funds that you can use for the collateralized system of stable coins that we talked about previously, or for borrowing purposes where you will be charged based on interest. When you have completed that process, you will then easily be able to link and connect your crypto tokens and store them in the wallet for as long as you would like.

Four DeFi apps to know about

When it comes to decentralized finance, there are hundreds if not thousands of applications out there that all have one purpose, which is to allow users/ individuals to store their personal assets of crypto coins, stable coin and physical assets like gold or silver, which have an equal value to any coins on the market.

ONE THING that is common amongst all of these apps is that you will find a decentralized exchange system or DEX for short, as we discussed before which is a a peer to peer-based system where transactions can be done safely between crypto traders without the need for financial institutions. So let's take a look at the four most commonly used and reliable decentralized finance apps.

Aave

. . .

BY FAR, one of the most popular decentralized projects/apps out there is the Aave which is widely known for its feature of allowing safe lending or borrowing transactions between traders of the crypto world. This platform allows users to trade via the system of smart contracts through its own pool.

THE GREAT THING about this platform is that it is built on the Ethereum network, which is one of the most popular digital networks out there. With the help of Aave, you do not need to pay any financial institution, finance manager, banker, or anyone who works in the finance system as smart contracts in Aave is able to manage the assets by making the users rely on a series of algorithms or digital patterns. At the current time, this platform has up to 26 different cryptocurrencies available to be used where profit can be earned.

Colony Lab

COMING in second in the apps of decentralized finance is the colony lab which is on one of the tops when it comes to successful and reliable DeFi projects. This project has received tremendous support from the Avalanche Foundation and hence has been able to set a firm ground in the world of finance. The amazing thing about colony lab is that it works on networks that have native tokens.

ONCE YOU HAVE the ownership of the tokens in the colony lab, you can then move them into a safe wallet, and from there, you have multiple options. For instance, many users out there choose to liquidate their assets so that they could profit in the form of interest on top of it. A large proportion of people in the finance sector have started to familiarize them and use colony lab as it is entirely community-based. If you are someone who has a keen interest and knowledge in the fields of momentum, marketing, networking, tech expertise, etc., then colony lab is just the perfect app/project for you to get started.

Pancake Swap

THIS NEXT TYPE of decentralized project is a relatively new one that is still emerging in the world of finance, but it has been able to attract many individuals out there. The pancake swap application is primarily based on Binance smart chain, and just like Aave, it is a trading liquidity provider platform. This means that you are able to use your assets and lend them to a borrower and so are able to earn profit through interest charges.

THERE ARE many reasons why pancake swap is a good and reliable project as it is built on Binance, which, if you do not know, is one of the world's largest cryptocurrency exchanges. Now you might be thinking, is pancake swap run and automated by Binance? The answer to that is no, pancake swap operates with a system of finance, but it allows users to lend their crypto tokens without ever losing the authority over them.

MOREOVER, pancake swap uses an automated model called AMM, which makes the process of depositing funds easier. When users deposit their funds, they get tokens called LP tokens which you can use to gain back a share/part of trading fees, hence locking your crypto tokens in the pool to earn maximum profit. Another unique concept of pancake swap is the reward system of "cake" tokens which users get when they first get their LP tokens and afterward earn "SYRUP" tokens which are used to get functionality such as governance tokens or lottery ticket tokens.

FANTOM

THIS LAST TYPE of decentralized finance application/project is a unique one as it is an alternative to the Ethereum network that provides smart contracts. If you are unaware, Ethereum is the first network to ever provide smart contracts, and this resulted in congestion issues as well as high transaction fees, but with the arrival of fantom, this issue has since become negated.

THE GREAT THING about fantom is that it provides a simpler way for individuals to borrow, lend and systematically make transactions. The core element of fantom is that it handles hundreds of thousands of transactions in just a second and is comparatively cheaper and faster than other networks out there.

SO THAT IS all for this chapter, guys! Let's change the topic a bit by moving to the eleventh chapter of the book, which is all about the risk management that comes with decentralized finance.

11

DECENTRALIZED FINANCE RISK MANAGEMENT

Throughout the course of this book, we have talked about the major pros that are related to decentralized finance, as well as some DeFi platforms where you can invest and earn profit. In this chapter, though, we will be focusing only on the risk management that is involved when working with DeFi.

ONE THING that you should know is that in any business or corporation, there will be some set of risks involved, and although these cons are not good for any company or business, they can be used to upgrade themselves.

AS THE WORLD shifted due to the dramatic effect of Covid 19, many businesses and institutions came to a halt, which in turn caused a decline in the economic growth rate. Every country, whether it be established or underdeveloped, had to deal with major issues involving the financial sector.

. . .

HOWEVER, between 2020 and 2021, large companies and people of value and power came together to create this platform which, to their and others' surprise, grew instantly to become one of the most talked-about projects. Today, there are so many projects that involve decentralized finance that makes DeFi a reliable and successful form of the financial system. In this chapter, though, we will be talking about some risks that are involved with decentralized finance and how they influence growth. So without any further delay, let's get into it.

The Popularity of Decentralized Finance

Many people out there are beginning to hear about the elements and growth of decentralized finance, but one question that remains in the minds of many is how successful is it and what risks are involved that could potentially cause its breakdown?

WELL, as of June 2021, the protocols which involve borrowing and lending have accounted for almost 18 – 20% of the overall device market. This is a huge success for both the people and the economy.

LIKE WE ALL KNOW, DeFi has created a bridge between investors without involving any intermediary like bankers, financial institutions, or any other person working in the finance field. Without the need of any middle man, any person looking to either invest, take loans, have insurance, or any other reasons could do so in a safe and efficient manner.

. . .

No one likes to go through the multiple staged process of collecting documents, submitting them, paying extra fees, and much more just to get one thing done. This is why decentralized finance is extremely popular as it eliminates the need for these requirements and also has been able to develop trust in its customers through its unique and new digital system.

Overall though, it is a good platform for people to come and gain profit through the use of assets; there are some questions that are associated that could cause this entire financial system to come to a decline.

Risk of High-Interest Rates

As we have mentioned earlier in the book, decentralized finance uses a protocol such as borrowing and lending for users to lend their assets that they own to someone who needs them with an interest rate. Now, although this is a good opportunity for various individuals around the world to earn profit over the assets they currently own, there is one risk involved in it that many simply are not talking about.

As new cryptocurrency projects are starting to come into the marketplace, the overall value of these coins is beginning to increase, which is something that not everyone can afford. Now this means that only a certain high standard population can afford to own these tokens and use them to charge high-interest rates when giving to other borrowers.

Although the overall system of decentralized finance is built to accommodate the needs and use of every individual regardless of their financial situation and background, this potential risk should be highlighted so that in the future, DeFi is not controlled and administered by high-class individuals only. While this is a potential risk, it seems like there is little to nothing that people of no power can do as more and more companies are creating projects of digital assets, which in turn are bought and owned by people who can afford these prices.

Decentralized Finance Rug Pulls

Although the decentralized finance platform is built on a promise to help not only lenders but also borrowers to earn a certain level of profit, there is still not a clear objective or level of trust where users could come in and use their valuable crypto tokens. Keeping this in mind, there have recently been multiple frauds or scam systems which involves the use of fake crypto tokens.

IN THIS TYPE OF SCAM, what happens is the developers create a new crypto token and automatically pair them with the existing one in the DeFi app, such as Ethereum, to create a new liquidity pool so that they can attract investors by promoting this token. When they are able to collect a certain amount of cryptocurrency, they use a form of backdoor helped by smart contracts that enable them to mint new coins, sometimes up to millions.

BY DOING THIS, these developers would sell their Ether tokens in exchange for the crypto coins that they have created, and once they have collected a substantial amount, they would leave behind these worthless tokens that have no value or connection to any company or marketplace.

. . .

ONE EXAMPLE of this type of fraud happened back in 2002 with the founder of sushi swap, Chef Nomi, who essentially liquidated his valuable tokens after successfully collecting tokens worth more than a billion dollars in collateral. Therefore, it is always important to have some background check before investing in these developers as it could account for a scam that ends up putting you in great debt and loss.

Impermanent Loss

When it comes to answering the underlying question of what are some risks associated with decentralized finance, the answer to that would be impermanent loss due to some obvious reasons. Now you might be wondering what exactly is impermanent loss and why it is linked with DeFi; the reason is due to the volatile nature of the crypto tokens.

EARLIER IN THE CHAPTER, we discussed some ways you could invest in the decentralized financial system, one of them being was by contributing to liquidity pools. The risk associated with this is that you invest your money and crypto tokens in the liquidity pools for borrowers to use and in turn, you are able to charge them an interest rate.

WHEN IT COMES to liquidity pools, decentralized finance has to maintain a ratio of between two risks, and this could potentially cause the value/price of the asset to rise or fall, thus disturbing the equilibrium.

. . .

FOR INSTANCE, let's assume that a liquidity pool has the ability to hold on to two tokens, ETH and LINK, with a fixed ratio of 1:5, so what this means is that if you are looking to invest in this pool, you would essentially have to depot ETH and LINK both.

BESIDES, there is another risk involved under impermanent loss, which is dependent on arbitrary traders who add in crypto tokens a value that is higher than expected. This can cause fluctuations in the actual value of the coin, and so it could potentially cause pressure to build up in borrowers, lenders, and other investors in the liquidity pool.

Attacks from Flash Loans

When it comes to understanding flash loans, they are simply a new and different type of loan that does not require the interference of collateral. The reason why this could pose a potential risk in the overall system of decentralized finance is that they use art contracts, which, like we all know, are the leading base to make all sorts of transactions.

ALTHOUGH IN THE CURRENT TIMES, the overall purpose of a flash loan is for borrowers to get it and, in turn, pay the full price of the flash loan in the same transaction. If the borrower fails or delays making the full payment back, the lender who has the flash loan would just take back the transaction, making it unsuccessful.

HOWEVER, one potential threat to this sector of the finance system is that there are many malicious and corrupt actors in the market who could use it to manipulate the people and the overall system. Not only this, but some actors could also use this flash loan to not only manipulate but also exploit the vulnerable nature of decentralized finance protocols, all for the purpose of gaining personal profits.

THAT IS why it is extremely important to be fully aware of which type of lender you are working with, and before building a contract, you should do a background check.

SINCE THE GROWTH of decentralized finance has skyrocketed before the imagination of the world population, it is extremely likely that some risks would follow it and try to corrupt this overall finance system.

HOWEVER, there are multiple other security measures being taken as well as investments being made to ensure the integrity and safety of decentralized finance platforms. So this was all for this chapter, folks! Now let's head to the next chapter and clearly outline some myths that are associated with decentralized finance.

12

DECENTRALIZATION MYTHS

Although the DeFi platform provides numerous benefits to individuals of all ages and backgrounds, it does have some set of risks. However, this is not something that you need to be worried about as every business, financial institution, or organization has to deal with drawbacks but what makes a company strong and useful is how they combat these difficulties.

THROUGHOUT THE COURSE of the book, we have gone through multiple times discussing the pros, cons, and potential risks that are involved with decentralized finance; however one topic that we have not shed light on is the myths that surround DeFi. Not many people know this, but decentralized finance, since its release back in 2018, has been able to surpass more than two trillion dollars, and it seems like, with its growth rate, this value is not going to stop increasing.

.   .   .

AS THE WORLD of decentralized finance is growing at a rather rapid pace, it is worth looking at some myths that people around the world have assumed. Therefore without any delay, let's get right into it.

Transactions on Blockchain Eliminate Risks

Although the overall foundation on which a decentralized finance system is built relies heavily on the need for peer-to-peer lending/borrowing without the need for any third-party interference, there are; however some risks involved that need to be highlighted. Now, where did this myth arise from, and how is it connected to the transactions made in decentralized finance?

WELL AS WE all know that blockchain uses so many distinct sources and features to verify and safely record all sorts of transactions made, there is a possibility that some of this data gets leaked or mishandled by the system itself. Although the DeFi platform users and large corporations who handle the growth of decentralized finance have stated that it is safer than centralized finance as no information is being shared with a third party person, it still should be kept in mind that systems can sometimes have issues.

IF WE LOOK at the traditional form of systems that have been around for decades, we can say that there have been new and upcoming ways to prevent fraud and corruption through the use of double authentication, personal passwords/pin codes, signatures, facial identification, and much more.

. . .

WHILE ALL OF this is used to prevent disturbance in the flow of the system, there is still a chance that hackers can automatically link individuals' accounts with theirs. Keeping this in mind, it is possible for fraud to occur with the DeFi system as, at the end of the day, the entire system relies on your ability to remember your password and user name.

ALTHOUGH IT IS A MYTH, unfortunately, this issue did come true back when coin base was hacked by gaining entry into the system and wiping away all the data stored by individuals who use coin base. It ultimately left them with nothing and no chances of retracing and recovering their personal funds/assets.

DeFi Equals the End of Banks

By far, one of the most commonly talked about myths that surround the world today is that with the use of decentralized finance, there is no need to use banks and other financial institutions where the personal finances of every individual are handled by a professional third-party/middle man.

ALTHOUGH THIS ASSUMPTION regarding the ending of the physical banking system is true to some extent as digital assets and funds are becoming more and more useful in many countries, it cannot be said that without the traditional finance system, people would be able to better manage their finances. Why, you may ask?

THE PRIMARY REASON behind this is that not everyone can handle their finances with care and responsibility as certain factors such as background, knowledge, use of marketing tactics, and much more come into play. Therefore, although this traditional finance system takes more time and effort to make transactions, there have been recent developments made by companies and authorities to speed up and modernize the overall financial system.

Completely Anonymous

When decentralized finance came into the picture of the overall finance system back in 2018, it attracted a large population through its unique features, which allows every individual to make transactions in the form of lending and borrowing without having to give personal data and information.

WITH A CENTRALIZED FINANCIAL SYSTEM, you as a person have to give all your relevant data and information regarding your finance to the authority so that they can manage your finances, and in return, you would have to pay a fixed service fee.

Now, although many people out there who are new to decentralized finance believe that it is completely autonomous and that there is little to no chance of information being leaked, there is some possibility to it. The reason why this is a popular myth is that all transactions made in the system are saved despite you not giving personal details.

FOR INSTANCE, when you are signing up for an account, you may not need to provide identity authentication, but once you make a transaction, the data related to it will be stored and can be viewed by any individual who is able to get access to it.

. . .

SINCE THIS DATA can be seen by a person, a central authority such as a government can easily trace it back to a bank where funds have been used to make transactions in the DeFi platform. To conclude, although the overall system where transactions are made cannot be viewed directly by any authority, it can, however, be used to trace back to secondary links like banks or any other financial institutions to confirm your identity.

Flow of Fake Crypto Tokens

Another major myth that recently has been circulating around is that many developers out there that use decentralized finance are providing fake crypto tokens to other investors, which ends up having no value in the marketplace. Earlier in the book, we discussed how this form of fraud occurs as developers own these fake coins and lend them out in a liquidity pool.

WHEN THESE COINS are borrowed by other investors, a set of interest is charged through which the owners of these fake coins benefit. Once their work is done, they completely vanish out of the pool, leaving behind these fake coins and taking with them crypto tokens that are, in fact, valuable.

PERHAPS YOU MIGHT BE THINKING, how can someone prevent from getting scammed by these developers? Well, the answer to that is that when you are making investments, try to engage and select large tokens which are at the top of liquidity pools.

· · ·

ONE THING that many people do is run a circle check where you essentially go through all the cycles with the crypto coin to see how the system of lending, borrowing, and charging interest is applied, and once you are satisfied, you can then start putting in a significant amount.

High Network Fees

It is clear that the decentralized finance platform itself is free and does not come with any services charges; there are, however, some network fees that you have to pay in order to use the features. For instance, let's assume that you are someone who is looking to start working with Ethereum through a decentralized financial system.

NOW IN ORDER TO interact with the smart contracts in the Ethereum platform, you would have to pay a certain network fee, and sometimes this fee can cost up to hundreds of dollars depending on how busy the system is. Although it is a myth, it can be said that it is true to some extent, as besides paying network fees, you also have to pay a certain amount to provide liquidity as well as to withdraw tokens.

HOWEVER, if you are someone who is only looking to explore DeFi and other digital platforms/ applications, then you could visit other blockchains such as pancake swap, Tron blockchain, just swap or Binance smart coins.

WITH THIS TYPE OF BLOCKCHAIN, you can easily explore the functions and elements of decentralized finance without having to pay an extraordinary amount of service fee. One thing that is worth mentioning while talking about fees is that, unlike other regular exchanges, in decentralized finance, you have to pay a commission by interacting with several smart contracts if you are looking to leave a pool.

Advice on DeFi

Although from the surface and looking at the potential profit you can earn with DeFi, it should be kept in mind that this type of financial system is best handled by those people who have vast experience in the world of finance and cryptocurrency.

IF YOU ARE someone who is willing to spend a considerable amount of money to get into the world of DeFi, then you should definitely do so after proper research and analysis. Some of the myths that we have previously talked about should be kept in mind if you are looking to start getting involved in liquidity pools, etc.

BESIDES THIS, another thing to keep in mind is that once you are in the system of the crypto world and decentralized finance, it can sometimes get challenging and risky, but if you think you are able to handle such risks and fluctuations in profit, then DeFi is just the perfect system for you.

SO THAT IS all for this chapter! Hopefully, by now, you have understood and grasped the idea of how decentralized finance works and what risk/myths are involved in it. Let's now continue this book by heading over to the next chapter, which discusses in detail some of the latest DeFi projects that you need to keep your eye open for.

13

DEFI PROJECTS

As you all are aware, there are certain levels of achievements that decentralized finance has been focusing on since its release back in mid-2019. Amongst the many features and elements of decentralized finance, some of the most useful and unique ones are the practice of ditching paperwork and the need to hire a middle man to handle and manage all your financial work.

SINCE THERE IS ABSOLUTELY no interference or reliance from any third person or person, you are able to securely complete a transaction in a matter of a few seconds. Now economically speaking, decentralized finance has great and bigger use in large companies and organizations but this does not mean that you as an individual are not able to participate for your own interest and profit.

WITH THE IMMENSE support and security gained through blockchain technology and application, you can easily have a safe and efficient flow of digital assets/funds. With that being said, let us look at some recent decentralized finance projects that have been introduced in 2021, which aims to transform the world of finance.

Cardano Project

Starting with the first project of decentralized finance, we have the Cardano project, which has been considered as one of the leading blockchain projects which solely aims to use energy protocols as well as proof of stake protocols. In recent times, the Cardano project has successfully invested up to 100 million dollars in decentralized finance, which not only opened the doors for large corporations and investment companies to come together and create unifying projects but also has attracted individuals from around the world.

IF YOU ARE unaware of the Cardano project, it is simply a new and advanced blockchain technology that was founded by the co-creator of Ethereum back in 2015, Charles Hoskinson. As of current times, the Cardano native cryptocurrency is ADA and is priced at a value of $1.64.

THERE ARE numerous advantages to this type of device platform as recently, in February of 2021, the team of developers has stated that they are working on introducing an update that will allow all the users to have complete ownership of their tokens and support stable coins with the help of traditional physical currencies such as USD or AUD. Many people of finance interest have already stated that in the future, the Cardano project will be able to surpass the success and growth achieved by Ethereum.

Polkadot

Coming to our second decentralized finance project is Polkadot which is built entirely on a system where independent blockchain systems can store and share information in a trustless way with the help of the system Polkadot relay chain.

Now what this essentially means is that in the future, companies and investors who choose to build projects on Polkadot could do so in a safe and faster way than Ethereum. When it comes to talking about the benefits of working on Polkadot, there are many, and some of them include having complete and maximum security when making investments and transactions.

In addition to that, the Polkadot works on a chain system, which means that information, can easily be transferred in a seamless manner to another blockchain, hence proving that there is no need to have any sort of middle man or financial manager at all times.

Furthermore, another benefit that comes with Polkadot is that it enables users of all kinds to process upgrades without having the need to make two separate blocks or transaction histories. This, in turn, saves not only time for everyone but also energy overall. Polkadot works on it by creating governance models, which has the power to customize the models according to their needs and terms of functionality.

Synthetix

This next type of DeFi platform called synthetic is a relatively new and evolving decentralized exchange that primarily allows crypto assets and tokens to be traded with valuable currencies, stocks, and other assets in the marketplace, which holds an immense value in the traditional financial institutions in Hong Kong, London and the United Kingdom.

ONE OF THE great things about synthetic, which makes it completely unique and unparalleled to other DeFi projects, is that it allows all users to safely mint their assets which are called "synths," and in turn gives them great exposure to fiat currency, cryptocurrency and other forms of assets that are valuable in the market.

SOME OF THE examples of assets that are being used in synthetic are Bitcoin, gold, Tesla stocks, Euros, USD, and much more. In a nutshell, synthetic has managed to evolve into a new and secure DeFi project which allows users to bet on any price of an asset without ever having to hold on to the actual assets.

SOME OTHER BENEFITS of synthetic include allowing users to have experience and rely on its technology which is called the oracle technology, which has the function of checking and tracking price movements through the help of smart contracts. Although this project is still in its developing stage, it can be concluded that synthetic has the potential to reach a new level of growth in the marketplace.

Terra Luna (LUNA)

Coming to our last decentralized finance project is the terra
Luna which is widely known for being a next-generation and
unique smart contract are built to have features that combine
decentralized finance and stable coins. Earlier in the book, we
have talked about stable coins and how different types of stable
coins can be used for the collateral system.

THERE ARE multiple benefits when it comes to this type of DeFi
project as it not only is about interoperability programming but
also that it has a transparent ecosystem. This essentially means
that it works solely to eliminate the need for complex finance
and complicated payment chains.

TERRA LUNA WAS FOUNDED BACK in the early days of decentralized finance in 2018, and soon after, it became one of the most
talked-about decentralized finance projects. The current price
of terra Luna as of February 2021 is $54.1711, which is around
47% less than the average price of a crypto token out there in
the market.

SO IF YOU are someone who is looking to get started with the
world of decentralized finance, investing in the coins of terra
Luna is the right and safe step for you to take. With that being
said, we have reached the end of this chapter. Let's head over to
the next chapter, which talks about smart contracts and how
they are used with decentralized finance.

14

SMART CONTRACTS

S o, at last, we have come to the fourteenth chapter of this book which solely talks about the foundation of decentralized finance, which is a smart contract, and how it works together to provide individuals the opportunity to maximize the use of their personal assets. When it comes to understanding smart contracts, it is important to first understand blockchain technology and how it works together in this digital form of system. In simple words, to recall what blockchain technology is; it is a system that has the sole purpose of storing information in a way that makes it almost impossible and extremely difficult to track, hack, and get scammed? The data stored in this blockchain technology is completely secure and transparent; hence it is distributed across multiple computers that accept the system of blockchain technology. There are countless benefits of blockchain technology that make it popular amongst other online projects like decentralized finance as well as for cryptocurrencies.

.   .   .

ONE GREAT THING about blockchain technology is that if one form of data is changed or slightly altered by someone, the changes and its effect would be seen on all other connected data, hence making it vulnerable. Now when people hear of this blockchain technology term, the one question that comes to their mind is what exactly is the difference between the typical database storage system and the blockchain?

WELL, the answer to that is quite simple as in the blockchain, data is stored in groups, called blocks, hence the name: blockchain. When a certain block is completed, it automatically connects itself to the previous block, making a firm and secure chain that cannot be hacked into.

ALTHOUGH, there is an array of different types of data that could be stored, the most common use of blockchain technology is used as a ledger for transactions. Now since that is out of the way, let's take a look in-depth at smart contracts and how they are related to this whole DeFi and blockchain topic.

Understand Smart Contracts

Whether you are someone who has been actively involved in this world of cryptocurrency or is someone who has recently started to research more, one topic that you will always come across is smart contracts.

TALKING ABOUT THE DEFINITION, a smart contract is a form of online self-executing contract that is made directly between the buyer and seller. It is written directly with the help of lines of codes and not any official middle man or authoritative figures like a bank or financial institution. Many people of power, including Nick Szabo, who is an American computer scientist, has made it abundantly clear that smart contracts are a new form of computerized transaction protocol.

THE MAIN PURPOSE of smart contracts is to simplify business transactions and trade between two common parties without having to introduce or go through the process of legal paperwork. Now that you have understood the concept of smart contracts let's take a look in detail at how smart contracts actually work.

Workings of Smart Contracts

The core element on which smart contracts are based is through the is/when/then code which is directly written into blockchain technology. Once codes and verification of certain data between two parties who are looking to make a transaction have been completed, the next step would be the computers executing it.

THE ACTIONS that these computers include are safely releasing funds to other appropriate parties, sending notifications related to private information, registering a ticket, and much more. After everything has been completed, the blockchain would then be automatically completed to ensure that the transaction does not change at all.

OVERALL THOUGH, the use of smart contracts extend over exchanges of goods, real estate, securities, and other digital and physical assets which have a value equivalent to digital assets.

From the surface, it may seem like a risky thing to invest time, effort, and money in, but that is not a entirely true as all the contracts made are stored and replicated in a decentralized way so that no one other than the relevant parties can access and use it. Although the world is moving towards using physical assets which have a value equivalent to a digital asset, it is still a challenging thing to do.

Advantages of Smart Contracts

So now that you know how smart contracts really operate, let's take a look at some of the major advantages they offer to every individual working on decentralized finance. By far, one of the unique advantages of smart contracts is that it is fast, which means that processing data and documents takes a small amount of time as it is automated and digitally performed.

WITH SMART CONTRACTS, there is complete independence in terms of as it rules out the interference from any third party person/authority. With a centralized financial system, there is a higher chance of errors occurring during the execution process, but this is not the case with smart contracts, as the automated system itself is designed to minimize the risk of error and fraud. In addition to that, it is worth mentioning that smart contracts actually help you save money as there is no need to pay a service fee for any middle man or financial institution.

Drawbacks of Smart Contracts

Although the system of smart contracts is built to provide users with complete reliability, the reason behind this is due to the blockchain, which stores data that cannot be altered by anyone or destroyed. If, for instance, one party is not able to fulfill the requirements of a project/transaction, the system will automatically protect the conditions and information of the other party.

WITH THAT BEING SAID, there are, however, a few drawbacks that are worth looking at. One of them being is the difficulty of implementation, as integrating the workings and information in smart contracts to real-world systems can take a lot of time, effort, and even money.

ONE IMPORTANT THING worth mentioning is the smart contracts pros, and its con is that parties are not able to change or modify smart contracts if a new plan has been put forth by the party members. Hence both parties need to agree on one thing and stick to it throughout the entire project.

HERE LIES the end of the fourteenth chapter of this book! It is high time that we head over to the fifteenth chapter of the book, which talks all about how peer-to-peer lending systems work and the benefits that they provide.

15

PEER TO PEER LENDING NETWORKS

E arlier in the book, we slightly touched on peer-to-peer lending networks and how they are used on decentralized finance to eliminate the need for any middle man or help from any banker/financial institution.

IN PEER-TO-PEER LENDING NETWORKS, users/different parties have the ability to obtain loans directly from another party without having to go through all the requirements and processes that you would take traditionally with banking systems.

FOR INSTANCE, let's assume that you are someone who wants to take out a loan of fifty thousand dollars, and so you go to a bank, and one of the employees helps you get started by reviewing your current finances/personal history and so much more before they transfer you to a central authority from where you could get the loan.

· · ·

ON THE OTHER HAND, if you are using decentralized finance, you will not be able to have to go through the needs and processes of all that and can directly get a loan from another party. The element on which this is based is your current assets and history of clearance. Many people also like to refer to peer-to-peer lending networks as "social lending" or "crowd lending" as it helps people with social interaction while making transactions, thus creating business. Let's get into this chapter and learn more about the workings of peer-to-peer lending networks and some of the advantages it offers to the economy and individuals working in decentralized finance.

Workings of Peer to Peer Lending Networks

The prime purpose of peer-to-peer lending networks is that they can connect those individuals who are in need of money or any other form of credit with those who are willing to lend. Most of the time, the lenders are investors working in large companies or authorities who charge their borrowers with a fixed fee.

ONE OF THE unique things about peer-to-peer lending networks is that you could easily register either as a borrower or a lender through the multiple applications out there. It is worth mentioning, though, that if you are a borrower who wants to register for lending purposes, you would essentially have to pay the flat registration fee as well as undergo a risk evaluation criteria/process so that you can be eligible for any loan/funds. Although, the majority of the peer-to-peer lending networks automatically give out lending offers to borrowers, there are, however, some applications where borrowers have to ask for offers themselves.

.   .   .

It can be considered as a form of business as your input is being linked and transferred to a lender, thus creating a direct chain between you and the lender. When it comes to loans, typically speaking, it varies from 10% up to 30% depending on how big the loan/ funds are and the amount of time it will take for you to give back. Once all the legal requirements have been checked and confirmed, the contract is signed by both parties, and thus loans are transferred.

Evaluation of Borrowers

One question that many people who are looking to register themselves as potential borrowers is the criteria needed by the system to be able to enroll in the network. When it comes to the requirements, there are not many, and the ones that are needed are usually checked and verified to minimize the risk of fraud and corruption in the system. It is worth mentioning that in peer-to-peer lending networks, the system in the platform does not evaluate a borrower's history by looking at their credit score, something that would be done in the traditional finance system by a banker.

The platform uses technology and a system to keep track of a person's credit history income as well as focuses more on the borrower's public social interactions such as social media activity, media usage, searches, and much more. This shows how reliable and secure this network of the system is compared to the centralized system of finance out there.

After the platform has collected the data and information of the borrower, the next step would be to create a risk bucket, depending on how big the loan is. Usually though, borrowers would be given the opportunity to pay the interest fee or have the potential lenders bid on an array of interest rates.

Risks and Lenders

It is important to know that lenders usually use this form of a network system as it completely eliminates the prescribed criteria that would be needed for traditional lenders. The overall safety system relies on the risk management associated with peer-to-peer lending networks.

So the question that arises is how risky is it to give loans to borrowers? Although a background check is done to make sure that the borrower is safe and verified, this does not mean that there are no risks associated with paying back the loan. The reason why this is a potential risk is that the loans are unsecured and not backed up by a central authority figure; hence the chances of the borrower not paying back the loan are relatively high.

However, on the bright side, it should be noted that in this system, all the details of the borrower, including the personal identity, amount of loan taken, credit score, and interest rate, is shared with the lender once the contract is signed by both parties. Only the borrower's private identity and personal information are shared and given to the lender, but no information is disclosed regarding the lender.

Safety Measure

If you are someone who is worried about the privacy and integrity of the borrower during lending a loan, then you have nothing to worry about as there are several security measures that you could take to ensure complete security. It is important to always check the interest rate on the offer you are making so that in case there are changes made to the bidding system, you are aware and can have the maximum profit that you deserve.

BEFORE FOCUSING on giving exposure to any borrower, it is best to always go to the borrower's profile and authenticate so that you know what you are getting yourself into. Lastly, it is important that once the contract has been made and the loan is given, you check and monitor on a regular basis so that you know where your loan is being taken.

REGULATION OF PLATFORM

SO NOW THAT you know of some of the ways you could take safety measures to ensure that your funds do not go into the hands of someone who is corrupt, let's take a look at how these platforms are regulated. It is worth noting that all users, regardless of their background, are required to register for a peer-to-peer lending license. There are multiple rules and one of them being is that no lender is allowed to put as much money as they like as it could account for fraud and corruption.

BENEFITS TO PEER to Peer Lending

COMING to this last section of the peer to peer lending system chapter, let's discuss some of the major benefits that account for its security, safety, and popularity. There are two sections of the benefits which are received equally by both the lender and the borrower. For borrowers, one of the prime keys to using peer-to-peer lending is that you can auction your loan to members who have funds to lend.

ONCE YOU DO THIS, any lender or bidder is able to see the information you have provided on the p2p lending system. As for lenders, there are numerous benefits, and some of them are that lenders are able to enjoy the interest money that they gain from allowing borrowers to have a loan. Not only this but lenders and borrowers are able to make a community that can create unique exchanges within the system that extends beyond the use of loans etc.

OVERALL THOUGH, the system of peer-to-peer lending is a relatively unique and efficient one as it allows you to have more control over your finances without having to pay someone to do the work for you. You, as a lender, can earn a profit when lending loans, and as for the borrower, they can use this money for other purposes such as investments, etc.

AS OF NOW, there are P2P lenders in several different countries such as Japan, Italy, China, the Netherlands, and much more. So here lies the end of this chapter as well. In the next chapter, you will learn more about the different digital wallets of decentralized finance and their value in the overall market.

16

DIFFERENT DEFI DIGITAL WALLETS

I n the previous chapter, we talked about how you can regulate the flow of funds in the shape of loans between two direct parties without ever acquiring the assistance of a middle man. We also went through some advantages as well as safety measures that you, as a lender, should take care of when processing loans with a borrower. In this chapter, though, we will be focusing more on the different types of decentralized finance digital wallets and how they are used by individuals to earn max profit.

As you are aware, the main purpose of having a safe DeFi digital wallet is so that you can keep all your assets safe. For instance, if you are someone who loves to engage in-game activities involving the use of cryptocurrency objects/items and wants to keep them aside in a safe place, then DeFi digital wallets is the best place for you as here you are able to keep all your assets gained from games/other activities and never lose them, even when the game or any other form of the activity itself has perished in the market. Let's continue on with this chapter and learn more about the workings and systems of different decentralized finance wallets in 2021.

What Makes a DeFi Wallet Successful

When it comes to DeFi wallets, there are certain elements that are put together to make the system itself an efficient and unique one. To start off, one of the key elements of DeFi wallets is that it is key-based, which essentially means that every user, regardless of their income, background, or finance history, will get assigned with a unique key that can be used to access their wallet.

GENERALLY, the key is in a 12 words phrase and is solely the responsibility of the owner to remember and safeguard it from other people. Furthermore, DeFi wallets are non-custodial, which simply means that funds can be transferred and received with full confidentiality as DeFi platforms give complete assurance to their users that they are the only ones accessing it.

THIRDLY, most DeFi wallets do in fact, come with accessibility features that allow users to manage a complete set of assets. Some of the most common and popular cryptocurrency coins that you can deposit are ETH, Stable coins like Dai, ERC721, and even some tokens from games like axie infinity, decentral, and, much, much more.

Metamask

Earlier in the book, we have discussed some decentralized finance wallets which are used by individuals for different purposes ranging from storage units to profits. When talking about DeFi wallets, it is pertinent to mention metamask as it is the world's leading digital DeFi wallet that is used by a large portion of the world.

ALTHOUGH METAMASK IS ESSENTIALLY a web browser extension; it could, however, serve the purpose of a wallet where you can store your personal assets. One of the unique things about Meta masks is that you can access them not only on computers but also on your phone, thus meaning that you can carry your assets in your pocket at all times.

METAMASK OFFERS flexibility in terms of its acceptance to a wide range of different crypto tokens and assets, such as ERC20 tokens of Ethereum, Binance smart coin, and much more.

ONE OF THE prime reasons that metamask has gained such popularity is because it offers support for polygon, which, if you are not aware of, is a multi-level/structured system where you earn profit. In the current times, there are many other decentralized finance applications out there, and the majority of them use the examples of metamask to illustrate the workings and system.

THIS ADDS to its uniqueness and popularity. If you are someone who is looking to invest time and effort in DeFi and other crypto tokens, it is best to start with a Meta mask so that you have a clear understanding of the system and the elements on which these platforms are built upon.

Coin-Base Wallet

Coming to our second type of DeFi wallet is the coin base wallet which, if you are not aware of, is also one of the leading digital platforms out there that allows individuals, especially beginners, to store their cryptocurrency coins as well other assets out there. The key feature of a coin base wallet that sets it apart from other DeFi wallets is that you only have to type in the name of the user you are looking to make a transaction with instead of typing out an entire hexadecimal code.

WITHOUT ANY HELP or assistance from other linked accounts, you can send assets to other users on the coin base wallet app. Moreover, coin base wallet is also preferred over other DeFi wallets as it provides a safe and effective assurance towards security by having biometric security, or a six-digit pin which only you are aware of.

Eidoo DeFi wallet

This next type of wallet, which has been considered as one of the best DeFi wallets in 2021, is Eidoo which is a multifunctional cryptocurrency wallet. One of the unique things about the Eidoo DeFi wallet is that it is non-custodial and allows the control of different decentralized finance platforms such as applications and other projects which are released.

JUST LIKE OTHER DeFi digital wallets we talked about previously, Eidoo also offers and supports different cryptocurrency tokens such as Bitcoin, Lite coin, ERC20 token, ERC71, and thousands more. Although this itself is pretty unique, it does not stop there as in Eidoo DeFi wallet; there is an in-built Non-fungible manager who essentially helps all users with different tasks such as borrowing, holding, purchasing, etc.

IN ADDITION TO THAT, users also get the opportunity to learn about various ways on how they could experience viewing of digital artwork, crypto-collectibles and other different digital assets in the marketplace.

ALONGSIDE THAT, users who acquired Eidoo DeFi wallet will also be able to get an EidooCARD which is similar to a debit card, but instead of having money in the account, you have cryptocurrency tokens which you can use to make purchases not only in the digital world but also in real physical life.

Argent

Coming to our fourth type of digital DeFi wallet is the Argent which has presented itself as a rather unique and radically improved cryptocurrency wallet as it allows users to not only have better control of their assets but also to allow freedom from the hustle and complexity of the paperwork, addresses, etc.

LIKE MANY OTHER digital DeFi wallets, Argent also has a mobile version that allows individuals to use the mobile version of argent, thus allowing everyone equal opportunity to access their cryptocurrency tokens at all times. As you may know, most of the transactions made in Meta require a transaction fee that needs to be paid, but with the help of argent, you can get relief from the transaction fee.

. . .

ALTHOUGH, these are all important features that make argent different from the other digital DeFi wallets out there, one other feature of this DeFi wallet is that it has a social recovery functionality called "guardians" that essentially allows every individual to get access to their assets in case they are locked out of it. This feature is a relatively new and improved one as most of the DeFi wallets do not have any alternative way for users to get a hold of their wallet back if they lose their pin code or username.

Trezor

Coming to the last type of DeFi digital wallet is the trezor which is regarded as one of the top picks when choosing the best DeFi wallets of 2021. The owner of trezor. Nikita Grubor launched the first prototype back in 2012, but it took some time for it to gain popularity and recognition. Trezor, unlike other DeFi wallets, is actually a cold storage wallet that comes in two distinctive types.

THE TREZOR one and trezor model T are the two different types of models of DeFi Wallet with different elements to them. The trezor one is comparatively affordable and efficient as compared to the trezor model T. However, these two models have their fair share of unique features; one thing that both models of trezor share are high security, which makes them 10x more reliable. In order to gain access to the trezor DeFi wallets, users have to put in a pin code that is specific and different from any other pin code.

MOREOVER, trezor also supports more than 1800 cryptocurrency tokens which is more than the majority of the different decentralized finance wallets out there. With so many crypto tokens, there is a high chance of hackers and other malware functions occurring, but this is prevented by the security feature of firmware signature verification. Overall though, trezor is an ever-growing and unique digital DeFi wallet which offers maximum security and multiple functionalities, making it top in the market.

So THAT IS all for the different DeFi digital wallets out there! Hopefully, by now, you can make a reasonable comparison between the different types of wallets and how they function effectively. So with that being said, let's review some challenges that decentralized finance is facing and how it could affect the near future.

17

DECENTRALIZED FINANCE CHALLENGES AND RISKS

L ooking back at the previous chapter we talked about and highlighted the major advantages to the different types of decentralized finance digital wallets out there. Although, different wallets vary slightly from each other in terms of their functionality and levels of security, one thing that is common in all these wallets, is the integrity of having your digital assets such as crypto tokens/non-fungible tokens, stable coins, and much more.

HAVING a safe and secure place where you can keep your assets is an important part when being involved in the digital system world. The reason for this is quite plain as there is no one involved within the boundaries of your personal assets; this means that you as an individual have the responsibility to keep them safe so that you can earn maximum profit in the future.

THROUGHOUT THE COURSE of this book, we have thoroughly talked about the advantages, potential future benefits, and other things that could help you as a beginner to understand the concept and relevancy of decentralized finance in the current time. This chapter, however, is going to be shedding light on the possible future challenges and risks that decentralized finance could face if things go slightly wrong or if the system is modified. So without further ado, let's get into it.

Liquidity and Market

To start off, one of the most commonly talked about decentralized finance challenges is liquidity and market. Now you might be wondering what exactly is liquidity in relation to DeFi and what possible downside does it offer to this whole system of finance? Well, the explanation for that is crypto tokens can be considered quite volatile and unexpected as their value can increase and decrease really quickly. One of the factors which account for the popularity and growth of a certain crypto token is social media; the higher the proportion, the more chances of it being top in the market. However, this does not necessarily mean that the value and demand for these tokens will not fall since there are so many tokens out there. It can be a challenge to have high value in the marketplace.

FURTHERMORE, if we take a look at the centralized financial system, it works through the system of leverage which limits the investor spending to maintain the right equilibrium in the economic system.

DECENTRALIZED FINANCE, on the other hand, works in an opposite way as users can come and participate in the auction of these rare and valuable tokens. If, for example, you purchase a valuable token that has cost you a great deal of money, if that token ends up unexpectedly dropping in demand and value due to some other crypto token in the market, you will be left with a loss and a coin with little to no value.

Legal Matters

Although the system of decentralized finance works to ensure that it is safe from any sort of corruption, both internally and externally, there are still some risks regarding the legal strictness and regulation. The reason why these legal matters come into the category of the potential challenge is that in decentralized finance, there is a lack of laws as well as punishments of any crime made against the system.

Since everything is based online, anyone could come up with suspicious software to corrupt the existing system. Not only that, but another major factor to consider is the practice of investors trying to indulge in transactions that are written off as banned, etc. This form of linkage not only damages the system of decentralized finance as it puts them at risk of fraud but also puts the money of those investors who choose to invest their time and money in jeopardy.

Risks with Smart Contracts

Although, the overall function of smart contracts is to establish a relationship between two party members, whether it be a lender and borrower or any other case, and eliminate the need for any third party interference, there are certain risks involved with it that could harm decentralized finance too.

. . .

ONE OF THE main risks involved in the smart contract occurs when you make an error in transactions, as this results in the entire project getting taken down, thus having to endure loss on both ends of the party. The reason behind this is that there is no involvement of any third man who has access to private and confidential information and documents, so if something gets lost or is slightly modified out of the plan, it could become irretrievable.

HOWEVER, it does not stop there; smart contracts themselves could have bugs as new leading projects make use of different smart contracts and bind them together. This results in bug problems in smart contracts, and although most of them can be fixed once the product and services have been made, they still pose a risk to the overall DeFi systems.

MOREOVER, there are also risks such as oracles which are necessary to execute safe and secure smart contracts which rely only on external data. This means that the information is coming from an outside source, and this could cause oracles to have faulty issues and that in turn may lead to malicious activity, thus affecting the execution of smart contracts.

Technological Threat

By far, one of the scariest and most damaging challenges that decentralized finance could face is hacking. The system on which decentralized finance and blockchain technology is built has been verified as a secure and safe one, but that does not mean that it can act as a shield against any new software.

· · ·

AS THE VALUE and use of decentralized finance by not only individuals but large companies and corporations are beginning to increase, hackers are bound to come in the way and get confidential information that could benefit them. Since there is no direct involvement from a third party such as a bank or other financial institution that would take the responsibility if your account gets hacked or modified, this essentially puts the users of DeFi at risk.

NOT ONLY THAT, but the introduction of new technology alongside smart contracts such as para chain, cross chains, side chains, and bridges has a different software base to the existing system, which technically means that it could easily get hacked or the information stored within this technology can be lost permanently in the system, resulting in a great loss for parties and investors.

Authority Control

Although, new platforms and applications that are being developed in decentralized finance work without the need for a middle man or authoritative figure, there may be a few times where a person or group of people will be in control before the entire project becomes decentralized.

SOME OF THE stages where this could happen are development, publications, deployment, and operation. In these individual stages leading to a project or service being decentralized, there will be times when a person could be in charge of controlling and managing the information provided by individuals in the party. Though the information shared and used is completely confidential and does not necessarily mean that it can get corrupted, there are, however, chances that should not be ignored.

So THAT IS all for this chapter, folks! It can be concluded that decentralized finance is a new and upcoming finance system that offers countless benefits to all, regardless of their age, finance history, background, and knowledge.

HOWEVER, it must not be forgotten that the risks that we talked about could account for a complete change in the way people view this system and how it works to benefit everyone. Since we have cleared that, let's now move on to the eighteenth chapter of this book which talks about the money transfer system in decentralized finance.

18

MONEY TRANSFER WITH DEFI

S o finally, we have reached this part of the book, which solely talks about the part where money is involved during the execution of new projects within a decentralized financial system. However, there are many people out there that know a lot about the working and benefits of decentralized finance but lack knowledge and understanding of money transfer.

THIS MAY SEEM like an easy task that can be performed by anyone; it is indeed something that needs attentiveness and the right state of mind. As we have mentioned earlier in the book, there are many hackers and software built by these corrupt parties to threaten the integrity and working of the system in DeFi, thus affecting its growth.

FOR THIS MAIN REASON, it is pertinent that before making any sort of transfer that involves money or even cryptocurrency, you know all the details and personal information. Once you do this, your chances of running into a scammer or fraud are likely to cease and will help you earn more profit.

IT CAN BE SAID THAT, like any other field of work, understanding and using decentralized finance can be a time taking procedure as there are hundreds if not thousands of available information platforms out there.

SINCE THERE ARE SO many to choose from, the chances of you running into the wrong hands is very likely. In this chapter, we will be taking an in-depth look at the main steps involved in money transfer so that you can effectively make transactions without any individual's help. So without any delay, let's get started.

Purchasing of Tokens

To start off this chapter, let's take a look at how you, as an individual, can purchase crypto tokens in a safe and efficient manner. One thing worth mentioning when it comes to cryptocurrency is that its value and demand change on a daily basis which means that you might be able to purchase crypto tokens at a reasonable price depending on the day, time, and marketplace from where you are purchasing it.

THE OVERALL PROCESS of purchasing tokens is not relatively difficult, but you do however need to keep in mind and be aware of what you are investing in. Instead of saving money on low-value crypto tokens, it is best to plan ahead on how you will make the investment, and then once you are prepared, you should go for it. There are many marketplaces that have crypto tokens with their own website link, meaning that you could simply click on the link where you will be directed to the official page.

To get started with crypto tokens, you should first download a coin base wallet app. If you are someone who is unsure of what a coin base wallet is, it is simply a self custody wallet that allows you to have complete access to your wallet and the information you store in it. One of the unique things about coin base wallets is that it comes as a mobile app; as well as a browser extension. After you have successfully downloaded the coin base wallet, the next step would be to create a personal username that you can use in the future to access the wallet. While you are doing this, you have the option to keep it private or share it with the public, such as investors, etc.

Storing Recovery Phrase

After you have successfully completed making a username, you will be met with a recovery phrase which solely consists of twelve random words. It is worth keeping in mind that the recovery phase is, in fact, the key to your personal cryptocurrency, which means that anyone who knows about the key can use it to access and withdraw the crypto tokens.

Although it is best to keep it to yourself, many people have made the mistake of accidentally sharing it to other investors in a pool lending system which results in fraud and, ultimately, scams. Besides that, you should also keep in mind that applications such as the coin base wallet or Ethereum wallet will never ask for the recovery phrase on the app for security reasons; if you are asked to do so, it is probably a fake, made-up website by hackers to lure you into giving your information for the purpose of fraud and stealing.

Now that that's out of the way, the next important step is to have money saved aside for paying fees and transaction service fees. The fees that you have to pay actually depend on many external factors, such as how busy a network is, the number of investors, the size of pools, the value of crypto tokens, and much more.

Transferring Tokens

For the purpose of understanding, we will be taking a look at how you can transfer crypto tokens such as ETH into a coin base wallet. So in order to do this, you would have to open the coin base wallet app from a browser, and from there, you should click on the "add funds" icon.

After you do this, you can then select "connect" under your coin base account. The next step would be to simply follow the step by step instructions that would be given to you on the web page itself. If you are choosing to purchase a crypto token, you would then have to click on the option of "make payments," where you can easily transfer real-life funds by connecting your debit/credit card information on the website.

Synthetic Derivatives

If you are someone who is unsure of what the term synthetic derivatives mean and what value does it hold in the overall finance market, then you should definitely learn. In simple words, as of now, there is more than 24 billion dollars worth of tether coins which are stable coins that are pegged to the US dollar.

Now, these forms of stable coins, as we all know, are circulated in the world of digital finance, going from one investor to another. Although these hold immense value and they can be stored so that their value in terms of US currency rises, there is the use of synthetic derivatives, which can be considered as an asset trading platform that allows you to trade other forms of derivative products, which includes but is not limited to Bitcoin, US dollar, Stocks, ETF, Australian dollar and even gold or silver.

THE OVERALL PROCESS of transferring and having a hold of these derivatives is a different one as you have to essentially plug them into a smart contract of BTC which will be issued in a value that is equivalent to Bitcoin, the most popular and valuable of crypto tokens. Now you might be wondering what the potential benefits of synthetic derivatives are, and let me tell you that there are a lot. The prime role of synthetic derivatives is to mimic unlimited potential profit and eliminate the chances of loss or corruption that may occur during financial transactions.

Financial Services Sector and DeFi

Now that we have discussed some ways money is transferred in decentralized finance. It is now time to look at some potential benefits that DeFi provides to the overall financial service sector and how these implementations help boost the overall economy as we have discussed earlier in the book that DeFi uses the concept of lending and borrowing, which can be considered as quite a useful practice and tool.

NOT ONLY THAT, but in recent times, up-and-coming new DeFi platforms have introduced unique methods to help individuals save money. By simply plugging themselves onto different types of DeFi applications, lenders could use the services offered for interest, and this maximizes their earnings.

WITH THE HELP of savings and other positive features that define offers to every individual, they can use this as a way to do future projects that are based on a decentralized and self-controlled system. As in digital wallets, users hold power to keep their digital assets to themselves; individuals can use this concept to do new projects, which would help the economy through the flow and regulation of money.

AND HERE WE have come to the end of the eighteenth chapter of this book. As this book is coming to an end, let's take a look at one platform that we have mentioned throughout the course of this book which is Ethereum, and understand its features and relation to decentralized finance.

19

DEFI AND ETHEREUM

Throughout the course of this book, you may have noticed that we have mentioned Ethereum quite a few times when talking about the different digital platforms which have a direct link to cryptocurrency tokens. In all the previous chapters, we went through great detail talking about the different kinds and types of digital wallets as well as crypto coins that are used in decentralized finance to make transactions.

HOWEVER, in this chapter, we will be taking a look at only Ethereum, which, if you are not aware of, is one of the most popular and in-demand blockchain technologies, which offers its own smart contracts that can be used to make peer to peer lending transactions. So since there are so many blockchain technologies out there in the market, what makes Ethereum so unique and how has it managed to stay at the top?

. . .

WELL, in this chapter, we will be providing the answer to this question and clear all your doubts and information regarding the use and popularity of Ethereum. So without any further delay, let's get right into it.

Understanding the Concept of Ethereum

Before we dive into talking about Ethereum in relation to decentralized finance, let's take a look at what Ethereum really is and how its own system works. So like, we have just mentioned before, Ethereum is an open-source and decentralized blockchain technology that uses smart contracts to make the transaction. Besides Bitcoin, Ethereum has its own cryptocurrency coin called ETH, which is considered as one of the most valuable digital coins out there in the market.

ONE OF THE prime reasons why Ethereum is so popular is because it was released quite early when the whole world of decentralized finance was relatively new and upcoming. Using smart contracts completely eliminates the need for any middle man; hence transactions can be made anonymously and publicly.

THIS MEANS that anyone is able to view the transactions made, but no one can know/access private information which is stored on the blockchain in the form of a block system.

Workings of Ethereum

Now that you have a clear understanding of what Ethereum is, let's now take a look at how Ethereum works and what different types of services does it offer to its customers. For starters, we know that in Ethereum and a safe digital wallet, you are able to send and receive ether coins and store them. Some other platforms, such as coin base, allow individuals to even take complete custody and ownership of their coins, in this case, ether, so that hackers do not get in the way.

BESIDES THIS, Ethereum also has the function to allow the use of non-fungible tokens, which can come from different places such as online gaming/art exhibitions. These tokens that are in the form of art, objects, etc., can be stored on Ethereum. Another interesting feature of Ethereum is that it gives equal opportunity for individuals to use different digital apps to build, store, share, invest and even make social interactions, while earning a profit.

RELATION OF DEFI with Ethereum

AMONGST THE MANY features that Ethereum provides to its users, one of the highly used ones is the use of decentralized finance. Why, you may ask? Well, the reason behind that is quite obvious and common as the world of finance itself is shifting into a digital world, many people are starting to like the idea of having no involvement from any third party interference and instead make transactions fully by them and their other party's own control.

HOWEVER, although this is a unique and rather optimistic approach to handling finance, many experts in the finance field are starting to say that this could cause the image of Ethereum to fall. As we all know, Ethereums own coin, ETH, has been in the market for quite a while now, having stood besides Bitcoin in terms of value. However, in recent times, its share of the total value which is stored and locked in the DeFi platform has tremendously dropped from 100% to 70% in just one year.

WITH THIS IN MIND, another thing is that Ethereum is starting to lose its market share by involving the use of decentralized finance to make transactions as its competitors such as Solana, Binance smart chain, terra, etc., are also using decentralized finance systems. These competitors are starting to gain large amounts of money, which they are in turn using to boost their own ecosystem.

Pros of Ethereum

The overall design of Ethereum is to ensure that it is not only cost-effective and flexible but also that it is open to everyone in the public and can be a tool for different parties to make dealings/businesses. When it comes to its benefits, there are many to list, but some of the most effective ones are that it provides data coordination.

THE ETHEREUM DECENTRALIZED structure is designed in a way to allocate information and data in a safe and reliable manner. Besides this, the Ethereum network itself is a bulky one as it allows millions of users from all around the world to work on the network. In addition to that, Ethereum also gives tokenization which is used by large businesses to have a hold on assets that are stored in digital format.

. . .

WITH THE HELP OF TOKENIZATION, these businesses can fractionalize and benefit from physical assets such as real estate and also expand their product lines. Some other benefits Ethereum offers are interoperability, open-source, safe incentive layer, high scalability and performance, and rapid deployment rates.

SO THIS IS where the nineteenth chapter of this book comes to an end. Let's move on to the next chapter, which talks about the potential future of decentralized finance and how it can be used to change the world of finance in the upcoming future.

20

FUTURE OF DECENTRALIZED FINANCE

S o we have finally arrived at the second last chapter of this book which, unlike others, will solely focus on the future of decentralized finance and how its ever-growing success will change the upcoming future and generation. One thing is clear, which is that decentralized finance is an advanced finance system that, although it is in its early stages, still has the potential to grow and improve with time.

MANY EXPERTS who are familiar with the field of finance have stated that in the near future, there will be little to no use of bankers or any other financial institutions. However, this is a collective and overall reflection on the success of decentralization finance; in hindsight, though, there are several factors that play a major role in the overall development of the DeFi system. Let's begin this chapter and talk about the ultimate growth and future of decentralized finance, as well as the core factors which hinder its success.

Economical Imbalance

Before we start talking about the future of decentralized finance, we have to first take a look at the different countries and their development rate to determine the overall success rate of decentralized finance. Although the DeFi system was first introduced in the US, which is a developed country, its effect and growth have reached other parts of the world, but when we look at statistics, we are able to see that the implementation of decentralized finance system is merely implied in developed countries and not in third world countries.

THIS FACTOR IS MAINLY INFLUENCED by the economic growth of a particular country, and if we talk about third-world countries, they are yet to change in the near upcoming future. In order for decentralized finance to work as a medium for the overall financial system, leaders have to come together and introduce new projects to increase the value of underdeveloped countries.

Risk factor

Although decentralized finance promises multiple benefits, which includes the "no need for middle man" policy, complete ownership of assets, both physical and digital, transparency of capitalization, efficiency in terms of peer to peer lending system, pool management, and quick transaction, there are several risks associated to it.

WE HAVE ALREADY TALKED about the risks of decentralized finance in the previous chapter of the book, and so keeping that in mind, it can be said that those risks can be the reason for hindering the growth of decentralized finance. If hackers and other unauthorized parties are able to understand the algorithm of the system in DeFi, it might be inevitable to protect the confidential information and data stored on any blockchain technology.

Future growth

While there are risks associated with decentralized finance, there are also strong factors that act as a backup and barrier to prevent the downfall of this financial system. As we all know, in decentralized finance, individuals are able to make peer-to-peer lending by entering a liquidity pool where investors will liquidate their assets and can lend to a borrower on the condition of earning interest for profit.

ONE OF THE unique things about this is that different liquidity pools can be tied together and exist on different platforms. The potential benefit of this is quite an important one as one can access and enter different liquidity pools without the need for transferring large sums of money.

So, in a nutshell, it can be said that with this feature in hand, individuals/ large businesses or parties are able to save not only money but also time and effort. This is a huge advantage to decentralized finance, which is used in a variety of ways that could potentially cause growth in the future.

Building Future of Finance

So we know that decentralized finance has the potential to transform the way the finance system is being handled, there is still, however, one question that needs to be addressed, and that is who exactly will build this future of finance that we all are beginning to rely on? The answer to that is a subjective and quite complicated one as one's perspective and understanding may be different from another. However, one thing that is needed for the DeFi to grow is a community; what type of community is that, you may ask? Well, as everything is being handled digitally and not in person, there must be a way for people to interact beyond just making transactions of crypto.

BY HAVING a community that shares and believes in one system, we are able to create new technologies, projects, rules, and so much more. So to conclude, it can be said to some extent that in order for decentralized finance to reach new heights, there is a need for a central community from where plans/projects and much more are devised and implemented. So that is all for this chapter of the book. Let's move on to the next and final chapter of this book, where we will learn about some tips that you could implement while familiarizing yourself with the DeFi system.

21

TIPS FOR INVESTMENT IN DEFI

A fter going through many chapters, we have finally arrived at the last chapter of this book. Hopefully, by now, you have a better and deeper understanding of the whole decentralized financial system and how it operates. If you are someone who is looking to invest in the near future with the help of decentralized finance, then this chapter is just the thing for you, as we will be talking about some tips that you could use to begin your journey into DeFi.

FROM THE SURFACE, we all can agree that the whole workings of blockchain technology, smart contracts, digital wallets, and DeFi is confusing and daunting, but if you have acquired the right tools and a proper plan, then you can easily venture into this finance world without any hurdles.

LIKE ANY OTHER BUSINESS, there is a dark side that can cause things to get quite messy and so it is important to know about the risk areas and what you could do to avoid them. So without any further delay, let's get into it.

Invest in Projects

If you are someone who wants to make use of your personal assets by investing in projects, then you should definitely do so, but it is pertinent to only invest in those projects which are administered by a reputed organization/party.

SINCE EVERYTHING IS DIGITALLY CONTROLLED, there could be false parties/hackers that will attract investors with the intention of stealing your assets. Before making any transaction or agreeing to any terms and regulations, it is best that you properly do a pre-search of the project and its potential risks, as well as benefits.

Making of a Portfolio

Before starting to put your money up for any sort of investment, it is important that you start slow and build a portfolio that can be viewed by other parties. Now you might be wondering what sort of portfolio? Well, in order to attract investors and be included in profitable projects, it is important that you have a secure digital wallet, funds, dApps, etc. Once you have thoroughly researched the different types of DeFi applications and their use, you will be more confident and have a clear idea of what to do next.

Borrowing / Lending Strategies

One thing worth mentioning when you are making transactions is that in order to do so, you only need collateral such as a smart contract which will work as an intermediate to set rates depending on the value of cryptocurrency. If you are making transactions and have been asked to provide credit-debit card information, know that it is a scam as there is no use of third-party interference.

BESIDES THAT, you should also keep a close eye on the interest rate that you will charge or, in the case of borrowing, the interest rate that you are charged. The majority of the time in the lending protocol, there is a use of over-collateralization, which as we discussed before, is a way for borrowers to provide a guarantee to the lender in the form of crypto that holds a value higher than the actual loan itself.

Investing in Tokens

If you are someone who is completely new to the concept of owning crypto assets, then the best thing to do would be to have extensive research on the different types of crypto tokens being sold in the marketplace.

REMEMBER, not all tokens that are high in value will remain the same as fluctuations in value occur on a daily basis. Hence it is important that if you do want to invest for future profit, you do so on coins that are top in the marketplace. You could also invest in nonfungible tokens, which can be found on games in the form of items, collectibles, art, etc.

Interactions with Investors

Amongst the many tips that you could use, one of the most important ones is having a connection with a reliable and safe investor. The reason for this is so that you could not only earn a profit but also so that you can get more involved in the different types of transactions, etc. Having a friendly connection with someone with whom you have made a transaction is a good start when starting to familiarize yourself with the whole world of decentralized finance.

So HERE LIES the end of this book! Hopefully, after reading this book, you have taken something from it and are encouraged to get involved in the decentralized finance world.

CONCLUSION

So finally, after an extensive detail of decentralized finance, we have come to an end. The whole purpose of this book was to help you understand and navigate the aspects and elements of decentralized finance. At the end of the day, this is just a book, and although it can be used as a guide, it is, in fact, in your hands to make a change.

If you are someone who wants to invest and get involved in the DeFi finance world, it is extremely pertinent to not only have the right guide and information but also to have a strong sense of motivation, willpower, and most of all patience. One thing worth mentioning is that miracles do not happen overnight as they require constant patience, hard work, understanding, and the right mindset; without these tools, you may not be able to reach your desires.

If, after reading this book, you still have doubts and questions regarding decentralized finance, then we would suggest you go back and read it again but with an open mind. At the end of the day, this new finance system operates and depends upon your knowledge and tactics; without it, it could turn into a disaster.

It does not matter whether you are someone who is new or someone who has been involved in decentralized finance; what truly matters is understanding and accepting that there are risks involved in addition to benefits. However, this does not mean that you should not invest in it, but rather you should see it as a challenge and obstacle that could be broken down with your effort and willpower. With that being said, thank you for reading this book!